*f*inishing
touches

Volume B

finishing touches

Volume B

Samuela Eckstut-Didier

Prentice Hall

New York London Toronto Sydney Tokyo Singapore

PRENTICE HALL INTERNATIONAL ENGLISH LANGUAGE TEACHING

Acknowledgements

The author would like to thank the following people for their helpful comments and suggestions during the piloting of *Finishing Touches*: María del Carmen Asensio, Chen Su Yuan, Pablo Garcia Sanchez, Huang Tsui-Ping, Hiroaki Iwasaki, Aileen Li, Carmen Lico, Lin Ling Chu, Rie Oshima, Ramon Siy, Min Jung Suh, Yuko Tsukamoto, and Jeonghyun Yoon. Sincere thanks also go to Isobel Fletcher de Téllez for her insightful comments and for her help in securing permissions for copyright material; to Li-Lee Tunceren for her invaluable ideas and her willingness to help no matter what was going on around her; to Karen Davy for her professionalism and for the great conversations; to Shona Rodger for last minute support; and, finally, to David Haines for his encouragement and confidence.

The publishers are grateful to the following for permission to reproduce photographs and other material:
Barnaby's Picture Library: p.26R;
Bruce Coleman Ltd, UK: p.51T;
Bruce Coleman Inc, New York: p.51BL;
Colorific!: p.45 (McGrail), 52;
Sally & Richard Greenhill: p.73;
Robert Harding Picture Library, London: pp.20B, 29, 30L, 48, 60;
The Image Bank: pp.18T and C (Grumann), 78;
Popperfoto: pp.5, 8;
Steve Richards: pp.18B;
Science Photo Library: p.26BL (US Department of Energy);
Tony Stone Worldwide: pp. 26T, 30R, 31;
The Telegraph Colour Library: pp. 20T, 44, 51C and BR;
World of Leather: p.20B.

<None>First published 1994 by
Prentice Hall International (UK) Limited
Campus 400, Maylands Ave
Hemel Hempstead
Hertfordshire, HP2 7EZ
A division of
Simon & Schuster International Group

Designed by Jane Molineaux.

Illustrations by James Alexander, Mike Lacey and Peter Wilks from Simon Girling & Associates,Graham Bence, Joan Corlass, Janek Matysiak, Carl Melegari, PanTek Arts, Jane Smith, Rodney Sutton, Taurus Graphics, Harry Venning, Ian West

Printed and bound in Great Britain by
Cambus Litho, Nerston, East Kilbride

Library of Congress Cataloging-in-Publication Data

Eckstut-Didier, Samuela.
    Finishing touches / Samuela Eckstut-Didier.
        p.   cm. -- (Prentice Hall international English language teaching)
    Includes indexes.
    ISBN 0-13-106139-9 (v. 1) -- ISBN 0-13-300005-2 (v. 2)
    1. English language--Textbooks for foreign speakers. I. Title.
II. Series: English language teaching (Englewood Cliffs, N.J.)
PE1128.E346 1994
428.2'4--dc20   93-31263
                                                              CIP

British Library Cataloging in Publication Data

A catalogue record for this book is available from the British Library

ISBN 0-13-300005-2

1 2 3 4 5 98 97 96 95 94

Contents

SCOPE AND SEQUENCE FOR THE COMPLETE COURSE

BOOK A	TOPIC	READING	GRAMMAR
UNIT 1	**Do the Right Thing**	"A Homeless Man's $29,200 Example of Honesty"	1. Conditionals (possible vs. unreal) 2. Making wishes 3. Multi-word verbs
UNIT 2	**What Are You Afraid Of?**	"Anxiety and Phobias"	1. Defining relative clauses 2. Present and past participles used as adjectives 3. *May, might, can, could* to express possibility
UNIT 3	**People and Other Animals**	"Rock Around the Croc"	1. Past progressive 2. Present perfect (simple and progressive)
UNIT 4	**Crime Doesn't Pay**	"Maximilian Langsner and the Murderer's Mind"	1. Past perfect (simple) and progressive) 2. Conditionals to speculate about past time (including inversion and mixed-time conditionals)
UNIT 5	**You Are What You Eat**	"Chocolate"	1. Passive (including passive with *get*) 2. Causative *have*
UNIT 6	**Men and Women**	"Who Needs Equality?"	1. Gerunds 2. *Used to do* vs. *be used to doing* 3. Gerunds vs. infinitives

LISTENING	WRITING	VOCABULARY
Interview with man who went homeless for a weekend	A. Coordination B. Topic sentences (1)	Multi-word verbs
Radio talk show about stage fright	A. Subject-verb agreement (1) B. Topic sentences (2)	1. Suffixes 2. Words of fear
Interview with animal rights activist	A. Pronoun agreement and reference B. Paragraph development – logic	1. Dictionary skills 2. Proverbs
News report on El Pueblito prison in Tijuana, Mexico	A. Subordinate clauses (1) B. Paragraph development – ordering of information	1. Crime words 2. Nouns formed from multi-word verbs
Interview with author about table manners	A. Participial phrases (past participles) B. Paragraph division	1. Dictionary skills 2. Prefixes
Discussion about women in the military	A. Subordinate clauses (2) B. Paragraph development – supporting information	1. Suffixes 2. Homographs

LISTENING	WRITING	VOCABULARY
Monologue on the importance of technology	A. Fragments and run-on sentences B. Revising a paragraph	1. Homophones 2. Compound nouns
Commercials for products of the future	A. Subject-verb agreement (2) B. Outlining	1. Prefixes and suffixes 2. Adjectives of extremes
Monologue on time	A. Linking words (1) B. Introductory paragraphs	1. Prefixes 2. Suffixes
Interview with archaeologist who digs up landfills	A. Linking words (2) B. Concluding paragraphs	1. American English vs. British English 2. Synonyms
Story: "Timeless in Paris"	A. Participial phrases (present participles) B. Developing a story	1. Reporting verbs 2. Parts of the body as verbs
Discussion on parent involvement in homework	A. Parallel structures B. Essay development	1. Dictionary skills 2. Stems and affixes

Wʜᴀᴛ ᴘʀɪᴄᴇ ᴘʀᴏɢʀᴇss?

Tᴀlking Pᴏint

1 How well do you know your history? Work with another student. Match the inventors in Column A with their invention in Column B. (Note there are two extra choices in Column B.)

Now put the ten inventions in Column B in chronological order. When you finish, compare answers with other students.

A	B
1. John L. Baird	a) ballpoint pen
2. Alexander Graham Bell	b) bicycle
3. Laszlo Biro	c) dynamite
4. Thomas Edison	d) electric light bulb
5. Robert Fulton	e) jet engine
6. Guglielmo Marconi	f) laser
7. Alfred Nobel	g) radar
8. Wilhelm Roentgen	h) radio
9. C.H. Townes	i) (the first successful) steamboat
10. Robert Watson-Watt	j) telephone
	k) television
	l) x-ray tube

Rᴇading

Before reading

1 You are going to read an article about several inventions. Four of the inventions mentioned are the bathtub, the toothpick machine, blue jeans, and the vacuum cleaner. To which inventions do the words on the left refer? Check (✓) the correct column. (Note: Check with another student or your teacher to find the meaning of any new words.)

	bathtub	toothpick machine	blue jeans	vacuum cleaner
1. canvas				
2. denim				
3. exhaling				
4. inhaling				
5. iron legs				
6. particles				
7. sewing gear				
8. slivers				
9. wedged				

1

Inventors Anonymous

EVERYBODY **knows about Edison, Bell, and Fulton; their names are safely ensconced¹ in the halls of history. But what about Kohler, Hunt, Forster, Strauss, Booth, and Roper? Their contributions have all become a part of our daily lives, yet the inventors themselves**
5 **have been relegated to a virtual anonymity. Herewith, then, we celebrate those who historians, for the most part, have forgotten ever invented anything.**

Who has not touched bottom to a bathtub? Yet few could credit
10 Michael Kohler, who took about 10 years to realize what he had invented back in 1872. Kohler, an Austrian, originally created a big iron tub to use for cleaning the skins
15 of pigs. Later, he noticed farmers and their families were taking baths in them. In 1882, he added iron legs, and the rest is history.

Walter Hunt is the genius – and
20 the poor businessman – who invented the safety pin back in 1849. He took out a patent, but sold all rights to his pin on the very same day. Hunt only made $100 in the
25 deal, not much for an idea worth millions. And in 1887, while in South America, Charles Forster of Strong, Maine, noticed that natives used slivers of wood to remove food
30 particles wedged between their teeth. He invented the toothpick machine.

Levi Strauss went west to sell canvas to California gold miners for
35 their covered wagons, but his product did not sell well. Strauss then noted that the miners needed

work clothes and started making canvas trousers with some sewing gear
40 he had brought with him. Once the canvas was gone, he ordered brown denim, dyed the material blue, hired some tailors, and opened a factory in San Francisco. Blue jeans had been
45 born.

Cleaning crews, janitors, and all those who want their homes to be nice and neat owe Hubert C. Booth a debt of gratitude. He invented the vacuum
50 cleaner. In 1901, several inventors had come up with machines that would blow the dirt out of the rug and onto the hardwood floor. This approach

blew dust all over the place and didn't
55 really catch on. Then it dawned on Booth that instead of exhaling, the machines should be inhaling and sucking the dirt out of the rugs. Voilà – a vacuum cleaner.

60 Genius is often scorned, however. In 1868, Bostonian Sylvester Roper invented a two-wheel "steam motorcycle." For years he sought backers. He wanted to open a factory.
65 But he was considered a crackpot and was ignored. In 1896 – 28 years later – Roper finally found a patron who was willing to put up the money, provided he demonstrate his two wheeler on the
70 banks of Boston's historic Charles River. An estimated 10,000 people showed up on June 2 to witness the demonstration. Roper, then 75, climbed aboard his invention.

75 The crowd cheered as the motorcycle took off and moved faster and faster. Suddenly, it stopped. Roper leaned over and shut off the engine, after which he collapsed to the ground. He had suffered
80 a fatal heart attack. At 75, the speed – only a few miles an hour – had been too much for him.

There are no monuments to Sylvester Roper today, yet he was years ahead of
85 Henry Ford and the other big names in the automotive field. So here's to Roper, Kohler, Hunt, Forster, and all the rest – including Joseph C. Gayette, who invented toilet paper in 1857. They were
90 giants, and our lives have been changed because of them – we just didn't know it.

¹ ensconced: placed comfortably in a safe place

Guessing meaning

3 Answer the questions. Then guess the meaning of the *italicized* words.

1. a) Are the inventors Kohler, Hunt, Forster, Strauss, Booth, and Roper famous people? _____
   b) *Relegated to a virtual anonymity* (line 5) probably means: _____

2. a) When you take a bath, do you stand up or sit down? _____
   b) *Touched bottom* (line 8) probably means: _____

3. a) Do some inventors hope to make money from their inventions? _____
   b) How can they be sure that others don't steal their ideas so that they can get the money? _____
   c) *Patent* (line 22) probably means: _____

4. a) (Look at lines 50 to 55.) Did the machines that blew the dirt out of the rugs and onto hardwood floors become popular? _____
   b) *Catch on* (line 55) probably means: _____

5. a) (Look at lines 63 to 66.) What do you think Sylvester Roper needed to open his factory – money or good friends? _____
   b) *Backers* (line 64) probably means: _____

6. a) (Look at lines 64 to 68.) Did many people want to give Sylvester Roper money when he first came out with his invention? _____
   b) Did they think he had a good idea or a crazy one? _____
   c) *Crackpot* (line 65) probably means: _____

7. a) Was Sylvester Roper's invention a success before his death? _____
   b) *Scorned* (line 60) probably means: _____

Comprehension check

4 Complete the chart with the missing information. Put a question mark (?) if the information is not in the reading.

Invention	Name of inventor	Date of invention	Idea behind invention	Change
1.			A tub for cleaning the skins of pigs	
2. safety pin				
3.	Charles Forster			
4.			Made trousers from canvas material	
5.				Made a machine so that it would pull in dirt
6.			?	
7.				?

What do you think?

5 Discuss the answers to these questions.

1. How would you rate the inventions mentioned in the article – the bathtub, safety pin, toothpick machine, blue jeans, vacuum cleaner, steam motorcycle, and toilet paper? Have they been very useful, useful, or not very useful?
2. The reading on page 2 is part of a longer article. The other part also mentioned four of the following eight inventions.

airplane	camera	computer
matchbox	paper bag machine	potato chip
radio	windshield wipers	

Which four inventions do you think were mentioned? Why?
3. If you had the ability to invent something, what would that be?

Vocabulary check

6 There were eight multi-word verbs in the reading on page 2. Match a word from Column A with a word (or words) from Column B to find these words. (Note: You will need to use one of the verbs in Column A twice.)

A	B
catch	off
come	on
dawn	out
put	up
show	up with
shut	
take	

Now look back at the reading and try to guess the meaning of these verbs.

7 Rewrite each sentence by replacing the underlined words with a multi-word verb from Exercise 6. Use the correct tense with each verb.

1. I was angry because they <u>arrived</u> late.
2. It <u>suddenly became clear</u> to me after she left that I had given her the wrong information.
3. <u>Stop</u> the machine when you're finished.
4. The new fashions <u>became popular</u> right away.
5. If we don't <u>think of</u> an idea to solve the problem, it will only get worse.
6. He <u>left</u> before I could tell him the good news.
7. I'm going to sign papers so that I can <u>have</u> a life insurance policy.
8. My brother wants me to <u>give him</u> some money so that he can open a restaurant.

Language Focus 1

1 Read these sentences. Then answer the questions.

> **A.** Walter Hunt is the genius who invented the safety pin back in 1849.
> **B.** Few could credit Michael Kohler, who took about 10 years to realize what he had invented back in 1872.

1. What is the difference in punctuation in sentences **A** and **B**?
2. If the relative clause in sentence **A** was omitted, would you know which genius the writer was talking about?
3. Which sentence contains a relative clause that gives necessary information to identify the noun the writer is talking about?
4. Which sentence contains a relative clause that gives extra information about the noun the writer is talking about?

Now study the information in the Grammar Box. For further information, read Part 1 of the Language Summary on page 14.

Grammar Box 1

The relative clauses in the sentences below are examples of <u>non-defining relative clauses</u>. A non-defining relative clause <u>gives extra information</u>. The information in them <u>is not necessary to understand the topic of the relative clause.</u>

> It is as the inventor of the electric light that Thomas Edison, *who was born in 1847*, will be longest known.
> The jet engine, *which was invented by Frank Whittle*, revolutionized air travel.

The information in the relative clauses above is additional. There is only one Thomas Edison and only one jet engine. Therefore, without the relative clauses, we still understand who Thomas Edison is and what the jet engine is. Note that commas are used at the beginning and end of non-defining relative clauses.

4

2 Underline the relative clause in each sentence. Add commas where necessary.

1. On the morning of July 16, 1935, residents of Oklahoma City, Oklahoma, woke up and found on their downtown streets 150 strange-looking things which required a deposit of coins to park a car legally.
2. The idea for these parking meters came out of the head of Carlton C. Magee who was a member of the local traffic committee.
3. Solving the traffic problem for which this traffic committee was responsible was proving to be very difficult.
4. One day Magee came up with the idea of a timing device which would show how long a car had been parked and a coin slot to pay for the privilege.
5. Magee took his idea to a professor of mechanical engineering, Gerald A. Hale, who eventually developed Magee's idea into the parking meter.
6. Parking meters have never been popular with drivers who would prefer not to have to pay for parking.
7. However, parking meters, which are now commonplace in cities around the world have served in part as a solution to the traffic problem.

3 Make one sentence from the two sentences given. Add commas where necessary.

1. The man was once called "The Merchant of Death." The man founded the Nobel Peace Prize.
2. Alfred Nobel spent much of his life studying the nature of explosives. Alfred Nobel's name today is associated with the Nobel Peace Prize.
3. The Nobel prizes have done much to encourage the development of science, literature, and peace. The Nobel prizes are given each year on the anniversary of Alfred Nobel's death.
4. Even as he was setting up the Nobel Peace Prize in 1893, Nobel was trying to perfect the technology of artillery pieces and battle ammunition. He devoted most of his professional time and attention to perfecting the technology of artillery pieces and battle ammunition.
5. Nobel eventually became owner of the Swedish weapons company, Bofors. He had worked at Bofors on cannons and warships for the Swedish army and navy.
6. It was no surprise that Alfred Nobel was always interested in designing, manufacturing, and improving weapons. Alfred Nobel's father was also a weapons designer.
7. Throughout his life, Nobel never gave up the idea that he could make wars impossible by perfecting the technology of war. He worked on perfecting the technology of war for more than 30 years.
8. Nobel made many long journeys. During his long journeys, he wrote up to 90 letters a day on how to achieve peace throughout Europe.
9. Bertha von Suttner spent much of her life arranging peace congresses all over Europe. Nobel sent many of these letters to Bertha von Suttner.

4 Work with another student. Write a sentence about each of the people on the list. (Note: Do NOT include a relative clause in the sentence.)

1. a student in the class

2. a famous singer

3. a famous actor

4. a famous athlete

5. the leader of your country

6. a person who has recently been in the news

7. a famous person in history

Now exchange papers with another pair of students. Rewrite the other pair's sentences by including a relative clause in each. Finally, look at the rewritten version of the sentences you originally wrote, and check that there are no mistakes.

Talking Point

1 Rate the inventions 1 to 10 in order of importance (*1* being for the invention that has been the most useful for society and *10* being for the invention that has been the least useful). Then work with three other students and come to a group decision on the order of importance.

wheel	photocopy machine
radar	paper
transistor	electric light
dynamite	steamboat
microscope	telephone

Now add to the list the inventions in Column B on page 1 not included above. When you finish, talk to a student from another group. Compare your group's answers with his or her group's answers.

Vocabulary Development 1

Homophones

1 Homophones are words with the same pronunciation but a different spelling and a different meaning. Find the homophones of these words in the reading on page 2. When you finish, check your dictionary for the meaning of any new words.

Example: nose - *knows*   (line 1)

1. rites	6. genes
2. would	7. cruise
3. minors	8. blue
4. sowing	9. our
5. died	10. hear

2 Work with another student. What are the homophones of these words?

1. knew	6. too
2. no	7. won
3. by	8. wear
4. herd	9. sea
5. their	10. sail

Listening

Before listening

1 Circle the things you use in your everyday life. Then discuss with another student if the things you have circled have made your life better, worse, or have had no effect on your everyday life. What about the things you didn't circle – would they have a good, bad, or no effect on your everyday life if you had them?

light bulb

video recorder

pocket calculator

microwave oven

computer

quartz watch

Listening point

2 You will hear a man talk about how new gadgets have affected his everyday life. Listen to the tape and choose the statement which best reflects his opinion.

a) Because of the new gadgets I have, I can now do many things better than I could do them before.

b) The new gadgets I have have not helped me to do things any better than I could do them before.

c) Because of the new gadgets I have, I now do many things worse than I did them before.

Comprehension check

3 Listen to the tape again. According to the speaker, what effects do these things NOT have ?

Example: light bulb - *We don't read any more than we used to.*

1. microwave oven
2. video recorder
3. computer
4. pocket calculator
5. quartz watch

What do you think?

4 Discuss the answers to these questions.

1. What did the speaker mean when he asked: "Why is it that we always think new means better?"
Give an example of something you have gotten recently that you thought would make your life better. Has it had this effect?

2. The speaker said:
". . . we've been tricked for years into thinking we can buy all kinds of things which will help us and solve all our problems and which, when you sit down and think about it carefully, haven't really changed anything at all."
What examples, besides the ones the speaker gave in his talk, can you think of which show that this is true? What examples can you think of which show that this is not true?

3. The speaker said:
"I wish I had a gadget that could whisk me from one place to another without all the hassle . . . or do I?"
Would you like to have such a gadget? What do you imagine this gadget would look like? How would it work ? What might its disadvantages be for the individual and/or for society?

4. Make a list of the things invented in the past 100 years that you have in your home. Which three things do you think you could not live without?

5. If you could travel back to ancient times, what one item would you take back to use?

Vocabulary check

5 Answer these questions.

1. What aspects of language learning do you think are *tedious*?
2. Can you *figure out* in your head what 33% of $485.99 is?
3. Can you remember the last time you searched *frantically* for something?
4. Do you have to *wind* your watch or any of your clocks at home?
5. Are you always, usually, or not usually *punctual*?
6. What is the biggest *hassle* you face in your everyday life?

Language Focus 2

1 There are "hidden" relative clauses in these sentences. (The relative pronoun and the form of the verb *be* are missing.) Try to find these relative clauses and underline them.

1. There was a contest held in Chicago for young inventors last month.
2. The young people participating in the contest demonstrated how their inventions worked in a downtown hotel.
3. The first prize, awarded to a 15-year-old girl, was a four-year college scholarship.
4. The winner, a tenth-grader at a Chicago high school, says she hopes to major in engineering when she goes to college.

Now study the information in the Grammar Box. For further information, read Part 2 of the Language Summary on page 14.

Grammar Box 2

In a reduced relative clause, the relative pronoun and the form of the verb *be* are omitted. Look at these sentences from the text on page 2. The *italicized* parts are examples of reduced relative clauses.

A. Hunt only made $100 in the deal, *not much for an idea worth millions.* (=. . . *which was not much for an idea that was worth millions.*)

B. Charles Forster noticed that natives used slivers of wood to remove food particles *wedged between their teeth.* (=. . . to remove food particles *that were wedged between their teeth.*)

---

2 Decide whether the reduced relative clause in each sentence is right or wrong. Then correct the mistake.

Examples:
Gunpowder, invented by the Chinese more than 2,000 years ago, has had a great impact on the lives of all human beings.
right   (*Which* and *was* have been omitted.)

It is hard to imagine what life would be like if gunpowder, had a great impact on the lives of all human beings, did not exist.
wrong

It is hard to imagine what life would be like if gunpowder which has had a great impact on the lives of all human beings, did not exist.

1. Alexander Graham Bell, the inventor of the telephone, was born in Scotland in 1847.
2. Bell began his career as a teacher of the deaf, who came to work in the United States in 1871.
3. The telephone, now widely used all over the world, was invented in 1876.
4. The first words spoken over a telephone were "Mr. Watson. Come here. I want you."
5. Watson, who has been experimenting with Bell for many years to transmit speech from one place to another, first started working with Bell in 1874.
6. Bell sent the message to Watson, who sitting in another room of their workshop.

3 Change the relative clause in each sentence to a reduced relative clause.

1. Most inventions start as solutions to specific problems that are of interest to only a few experimenters.
2. Frequently technologies which are developed for one purpose find their main use elsewhere.
3. For example, the laser, which is now used in technologies such as compact-disc players and medical surgery, appeared at first to have only military and scientific uses.
4. One of the biggest problems for people who are working on inventions is how to keep their work secret.
5. This can also be a serious problem for companies that are involved in research.
6. There have been many examples of patented and successful inventions that were initiated by other companies.

4 Read the text. Underline the eight parts where additional information would make the reading clearer.

The inventions are famous – creating the first airplane, the phonograph, the electric light bulb, the telephone, the radio. But how many know that Thomas Edison's heroic rescue of a child opened the way to his electrical career? How many knew that a toy helicopter inspired Wilbur and Orville's[1] interest in flight? And are there many who know that it was in a small attic in London that he used a combination of old cookie cans, knitting needles, bicycle lamps, and extra radio equipment to make the idea of transmitting pictures over great distances become a reality? Would many be surprised to learn that Charles Townes made his discovery of lasers in Washington, D.C.? Who knew that a college professor's promise of riches to anyone led a baby-faced student to find a way to put the shining metal in every home? Hall[2] may not have been an inventor like Bell or Edison, but he solved a single problem. Not only did Hall become very, very rich, but he transformed the world around him. There are many inventors. In the pages are the highlights of forty-three inventors' personal stories.

[1] Wilbur and Orville Wright were the first to fly an airplane successfully.

[2] Charles M. Hall was the first manufacturer of aluminum.

Now work with another student. Make the story more complete by using the information below to add relative clauses. If the relative pronoun is necessary, decide which one (*that, who, whom, which, whose, where*) to put at the beginning of the relative clause.

> **Example:** . . . was about to be crushed by an oncoming train
>
> *But how many know that Thomas Edison's heroic rescue of a child who was about to be crushed by an oncoming train opened the way to his electrical career?*

1. . . . was brought home by Bishop Milton Wright to his sons
2. . . . are sitting in front of their TVs at this very moment
3. . . . could make aluminum cheaply
4. . . . was named Charles M. Hall
5. . . . had puzzled great minds for decades
6. . . . the modern world owes a great debt to
7. . . . follow

Now decide where to add this information as relative clauses.

8. . . . John L. Baird lived
9. . . . was sitting on a park bench staring at the beautiful flowers
10. . . . inventions were many

Now rewrite the reading. Change the relative clauses to reduced relative clauses where possible, and add commas where necessary.

Vocabulary Development 2

Compound nouns

A compound noun is formed by combining two or more words. Some combination types are:

noun + noun:	bath + tub	= bathtub
adjective + noun:	blue + jeans	= blue jeans
verb-*ing* + noun:	cleaning + crew	= cleaning crew
noun + verb-*er*:	vacuum + cleaner	= vacuum cleaner

The stress in compound nouns is usually on the first word. We say "<u>bath</u>tub," not "bath<u>tub</u>." Some compound nouns are written as one word (*steamboat*). Others are written as two words (*jet engine*).

1 Look at the tapescript on page 84 and find eight compound nouns. Circle the ones that are written as one word, and underline the ones that are written as two words.

2 Work with another student. How many of the 21 compound nouns can you find by matching each word in Box B with the words in Box A? (Note: The words in Box A may be the first word or the second word of the compound noun.)

Examples: *airplane   candlelight   toilet paper*

A	B		
air light paper	back bag bulb candle clip conditioning fare flash	force house line mail moon news plane plate	port sickness street sun tissue toilet towel traffic

Now write questions about six of the words you found. Read your sentences to another pair of students. Can they answer your questions?
   Examples:
   Question: *How did people use to read at night before there was electricity?*
   (Answer: They used candlelight.)

   Question: *Who was the first person to fly an airplane successfully?*
   (Answer: Orville Wright)

3 **Read these instructions. Then play the game.**

Get into groups of six, eight, or ten students. Then separate into three, four, or five pairs. You will need to have a die (or six pieces of paper with the numbers 1 to 6 written on them). One student in each pair throws the die (or picks a piece of paper) and moves the correct number of squares on the board. The student and his or her partner then need to think of a compound noun in which one of the words begins with the letter on that square. (For example, if a pair lands on *C*, both *vacuum cleaner* and *cleaning crew* would be correct.) If the pair cannot think of a compound noun, they do not get a point. (They stay on the square until it is their turn again, when they take another number and move to another square.) Then it is the next pair's turn. If players land on the same letter more than once, they must think of another compound noun beginning with that letter. The game is finished when each letter has been used at least once or after 20 minutes – whichever comes first. The pair with the most points is the winner.

Writing

A. Fragments and run-on sentences

Fragments

A sentence in English must contain a subject and a conjugated verb. Conjugated verbs change in form according to person, number, and tense. Thus, *I have* is a conjugated verb, but the infinitive, *to have*, is not. Look at these examples:

    S   V
Everybody knows about Edison, Bell, and Fulton.
This is a complete sentence because it contains a subject, *everybody*, and a conjugated verb, *knows*.

    V
Went west to sell canvas to California gold miners.
This is a fragment. It is not a sentence because there is no subject. To change this from a fragment to a sentence, add a subject – for example, *He*.

       S
The *motorcycle* moving faster and faster.
This is a fragment. It is not a sentence because *moving* is not a conjugated verb. To change this from a fragment to a sentence, change the verb to a conjugated verb – for example, *was moving*.

   S   V
Hunt only *made* $100 in the deal. Not much for an idea worth millions.
The first statement is a complete sentence. The second is a fragment because there is no subject or verb. To change this from a fragment to a sentence, add the second statement to the first: *Hunt only made $100 in the deal, not much for an idea worth millions.*

A sentence must also contain a complete idea. Subordinate clauses are not complete sentences because they do not contain a complete idea. Look at these examples:
Because Roper had suffered a fatal heart attack.
This is not a complete idea. We do not know what happened because he had suffered a fatal heart attack. To change this from a fragment to a sentence, add a main clause: *Roper collapsed to the ground because he had suffered a fatal heart attack.*

All those who want their homes to be nice and neat.
This is not a complete idea. We do not know what all those who want their homes to be nice and neat should do. To change this from a fragment to a sentence, complete the main clause: *All those who want their home to be nice and neat owe Hubert C. Booth a debt of gratitude.*

1 **Decide whether the statement is a complete sentence or a fragment. Change each fragment to a complete sentence.**

Examples:
He invented the toothpick machine.   *sentence*

While he was in South America.   *fragment*

While he was in South America, he got the idea for a toothpick machine.

1. The artist Leonardo da Vinci had many ideas for inventions.
2. Although Leonardo da Vinci is perhaps best known as an artist.
3. He was also a superb painter, sculptor, architect, poet, and composer. As well as a brilliant scientist and mathematician.
4. He studied under the artist Andrea del Verrocchio. Later worked at the court of Prince Ludovico of Milan.
5. While he was at the court, he planned improvements to the city and its sanitation system.
6. Thomas Edison inventing things all his life even though he only received three months' official schooling.
7. After he invented the phonograph in 1877, Edison put all his effort into producing the first electric light bulb.
8. The invention which made him famous.
9. By the time Edison died in 1931.
10. To be a great inventor.
11. Getting a patent from the government.
12. According to the information in this book.

11

Run-on sentences

Look at these examples:

A. In 1901, several inventors had come up with machines that would blow the dirt out of the rug and onto the hardwood floor, this approach blew dust all over the place and didn't really catch on.

B. An estimated 10,000 people showed up on June 2 to witness the demonstration Roper climbed aboard his invention.

Sentences **A** and **B** are both run-on sentences. They are written as one sentence but contain two complete ideas. A sentence contains one complete idea, not two. Two complete sentences cannot be joined with a comma, as in sentence **A**. They must be separated with a period.

In 1901, several inventors had come up with machines that would blow the dirt out of the rug and onto the hardwood floor. This approach blew dust all over the place and didn't really catch on.

Sentence **B** was probably more difficult for you to understand than sentence **A**. This is because the writer used no punctuation to separate the two complete ideas. The reader has no indication where one idea ends and the next begins. A period must be used to indicate this.

An estimated 10,000 people showed up on June 2 to witness the demonstration. Roper climbed aboard his invention.

2 **Decide whether the statement is a complete sentence or a run-on sentence. Correct the run-on sentences.**

Example: Joseph Nicéphore Niépce took the first surviving photograph in 1827 he coated a pewter plate with bitumen and exposed it to light in a camera.

run-on sentence . . . . . *1827. He* . . . .

1. The invention of photography made accurate images of any object rapidly available for the first time, it developed from a combination of optics and chemistry.

2. People have always practiced some form of medicine, early peoples used herbs to cure illnesses.
3. In the 19th century, medicine developed quickly. Much of the equipment still used in medicine today was developed at this time.

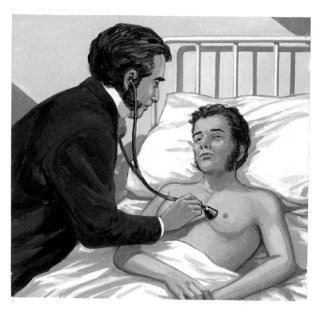

4. French physician, René Laennec, was the inventor of the stethoscope, in 1819 he created a tube through which he could hear the patient's heartbeat.
5. Blood pressure is measured by feeling the pulse and slowly applying a measured force to the skin until the pulse disappears, the instrument that does this is called a sphygmomanometer and was invented by Samuel von Basch in 1891.

6. By the 1850s, anesthetics were used by dentists to "kill" pain the first dental drills appeared in the 1860s.

B. Revising a paragraph

Good writers, even professional ones, revise what they write many times. It is during the revision stage that they have the opportunity to add new information, eliminate irrelevant information, move ideas around, connect ideas better, and change words. It is not a good idea to try and revise everything at once. Rather, it is best to focus on one area – for example, content and organization – and then rewrite the new paragraph and focus on another area – for example, style. Though students of English often think grammar is their most serious problem, it is more often the organization and content of their written work that is the problem. For that reason, correcting grammar, spelling, and punctuation mistakes should be done in the final revision stage.

1 Work with another student. Decide what the five problems are with the paragraph in terms of its content and organization. Then revise the paragraph and rewrite it. (Note: There are no grammar, spelling, or punctuation mistakes, nor are there problems with style.)

There has been a lot of progress in technology. Television has not necessarily had a positive effect on society. One cannot even say that the average television program is entertaining. While the educational programs children watch are beneficial, most of the programs are violent, boring, or silly. There is also the example of the computer. There is no question that writing on a computer is easier than writing with a pen or using a typewriter. It is easy to eliminate sentences, move ideas around, and correct mistakes. It can take a long time to learn to use a computer effectively. However, it cannot be said that just because people write on a computer, their written work will be of a higher standard. A good writer does not need a computer to write well. Thus, as the example of the computer shows, it is clear that in the end the only thing people can depend on to make their lives better is themselves.

2 Write a paragraph on one of these topics. Be sure to write an appropriate topic sentence that is not too general and is appropriate to the main idea of the paragraph.

1. Effects of technology
2. Life without modern inventions
3. An important invention

Language Summary

Part 1: Non-defining relative clauses

Example: Few could credit Michael Kohler, *who took about 10 years to realize what he had invented back in 1872.*

Meaning: A non-defining relative clause gives extra information. The information in it is not necessary to understand the topic of the relative clause. Thus, the relative clause in the example above gives the reader additional information about Michael Kohler. It does not define who Michael Kohler is.

Form: A non-defining relative clause contains the relative pronoun *who, whom, whose, which,* or *where,* and has a comma at the beginning and end of the relative clause.

Points to remember:
a) The relative pronoun, whether it is the subject or object, CANNOT be omitted from a non-defining relative clause.
> NON-DEFINING: The telephone, *which people all over the world use on a daily basis,* was invented in 1876.
> DEFINING: The telephone *I used* made a strange noise.
> The telephone *that I used* made a strange noise.

b) The relative pronoun *that* cannot be used in a non-defining relative clause.
> RIGHT: It is as the inventor of the electric light that Thomas Edison, who was born in 1847, will be longest known.
> WRONG: It is as the inventor of the electric light that Thomas Edison, that was born in 1847, will be longest known.

c) When the relative pronoun is the object of the relative clause and the pronoun refers to a person, the pronoun *whom* is preferred.
> Leonardo da Vinci, *whom many people regard as one of the world's greatest painters,* was also a brilliant scientist, mathematician, architect, and sculptor.

d) In formal English, when there is a preposition in a non-defining relative clause, the preposition comes at the beginning of the relative clause.
> RIGHT: The electric light bulb, for which Thomas Edison is usually remembered, was only one of his many inventions.
> WRONG: The electric light bulb, which Thomas Edison is usually remembered for, was only one of his many inventions.

> RIGHT: Walter Hunt, about whom you read on page 2, made very little money from his invention of the safety pin.
> WRONG: Walter Hunt, whom you read about on page 2, made very little money from his invention of the safety pin.

Part 2: Reduced relative clauses

Form: When the relative pronoun is the subject of the relative clause, the relative pronoun and the form of the verb *be* are omitted.
> Hunt only made $100 in the deal, *not much for an idea worth millions.* (=. . . *which was* not much for an idea *that was* worth millions.
> Charles Forster noticed that natives used slivers of wood to remove food particles *wedged between their teeth.* (=. . . to remove food particles *that were* wedged between their teeth.)

Points to remember:
a) To reduce a relative clause, there is usually a form of the verb *be.*
> RIGHT: The man who invented the parking meter never became famous.
> WRONG: The man invented the parking meter never became famous.

However, in relative clauses that do not contain a form of the verb *be,* it is sometimes possible to omit the relative pronoun and change the verb to its *-ing* form.
> Anyone *who wants to learn more about the subject* should read this book.
> Anyone *wanting to learn more about the subject* should read this book.

b) Reduced relative clauses can be defining or non-defining. If the reduced relative clause is non-defining, there must be commas before and after the clause.
> Sylvester Roper, *considered a crackpot by many,* could not find people to invest in his "steam motorcycle" factory.
> Roper finally found a patron *willing to put up the money.*

*F*UTURE PERFECT?

Talking Point

Discuss with other students what your hopes are for the future.
- For yourself
- For your family
- For your village, town, or city
- For your country
- For the world

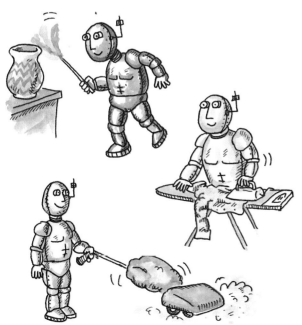

Reading

Before reading

1 You are going to read an article about the future role of robots at home and at work. Write + if you think the prediction will probably be true in 2019. Write – if you think the prediction is unlikely to be true in 2019.

1. Roboticized homes will become more and more common.
2. A robot butler will greet you at the door.
3. Little androids[1] will be scurrying[2] about.
4. People will be able to preselect[3] a frozen meal before they leave for work. At the appropriate time, the meal package will slide out of the freezer door into the microwave oven. When people return home, a hot meal will be waiting.
5. People's vacuum cleaners will roll out of the closet without any human help and do the week's cleaning.
6. People will have personal robots to do such things as take out the garbage, carry packages, and set the table.
7. There will be few people working in factories.
8. Factories will take up more space than they do now.
9. The main responsibilities of factory workers will be to give robots tune-ups, make adjustments if the robots need them, and be the robots' baby-sitters.

[1] android: something having human characteristics
[2] scurry: move quickly with short steps; hurry
[3] preselect: select beforehand (The prefix *pre-* means "before.")

A Day in the Life of a Robot

By 2019, the robot will be in the first phase of a tremendous evolutionary leap. No longer will it be a simple-minded, dumb,
5 unfeeling machine found only along factory production lines. The machine will have moved out of the cloistered manufacturing plant and into our world. We will work
10 alongside the robots, relax with them, live with them.

Roboticized homes will become more and more common. A first-time visit to one of these homes
15 might be a disappointment. No robot butler will greet you at the door, and no little androids will be scurrying about. In the household of 2019, the first phase of home
20 robotization will not be a single robot but a small family of intelligent appliances. (. . .)

Futurists at the Massachusetts think tank/consulting firm of Arthur D.
25 Little, Inc., suggest that the roboticized home will have automated centers where appliances are linked together into intelligent work teams. Getting a
30 meal ready, they say, could be simplified with a dual unit that's part refrigerator, part microwave oven. In the morning you would preselect a frozen meal stored in your freezer. At
35 the appropriate time, that meal package would slide out a door into the microwave oven. By the time you walk in the door at night, a hot meal would be waiting. If you are
40 going to be late, you simply call home and tell your home computer to delay the meal. (. . .)

Parked out of sight in a closet would be your robot vacuum

45 cleaner. According to a preprogrammed schedule, it would roll out of the closet, cruise over a premapped course on the floor, and do the week's cleaning. The
50 Japanese electronics firm Hitachi already has an experimental model of a robot vacuum cleaner that looks like a sleek, driverless car of the future. It sits quietly in the closet,
55 foraying out to perform its functions. Still experimental and costing ten times what current vacuum cleaners sell for, the robot vacuum will no doubt be part of some of the
60 more upscale, gadget-conscious homes in a 2019 suburb. (. . .)

By 2019, people may also first start buying personal robots (as distinguished from the domestic
65 housecleaning machines) simply for the novelty of it and for doing simple fetch-and-carry jobs. These small and unthreatening machines will be able to do such things as
70 take out the garbage, carry items, and set the table. (. . .)

We could control these machines in a variety of ways. The house computer might supervise
75 the comings and goings of all the smart machines. Or we could push a few buttons on a small control unit on our digital watch or the machine's torso to activate a
80 preprogrammed behavior. A simple way to instruct your family robot would be with voice control. Already, today's personal machines have voices, computer
85 memories, and even abilities like voice recognition. (. . .)

Life should be equally interesting for the robot outside the home, especially back in the factory
90 where it began. By 2019, it will be

the most common factory employee. The uniqueness of the roboticized factory will be evident as soon as you drive up to a plant.
95 While most of today's industrial complexes are sprawling acres of warehouses and manufacturing facilities swarming with armies of workers, future factories will be more
100 compact structures. They will have fewer people, and that will mean reduced space requirements: smaller parking lots and a lesser need in general for "people facilities" such as
105 lunchrooms and locker rooms. (. . .)

Rarely will there be a human in sight in the factory of 2019. Those who are visible will be there in a strictly subservient capacity: tuning
110 up, adjusting, baby-sitting. Of course, no worker will be allowed on the floor without his safety coveralls on. Emblazoned on the front and back will be bar-code patterns that warn
115 the worker machine, "Stop! A human is in your area." Since all the machines would have at least rudimentary vision, this should be the simplest way of protecting human
120 workers against death or injury.

Guessing meaning

3 **Match the words in Column A with their meaning in Column B. (Note: Be careful. There are three extra choices in Column B.)**

A	B
1. *dual* (line 31)	a) for people with a lot of money
2. *upscale* (line 60)	b) difficult jobs
3. *distinguished* (line 64)	c) moving in a crowd
4. *novelty* (line 66)	d) having two parts
5. *torso* (line 79)	e) in the earliest stages of development
6. *sprawling* (line 96)	f) of less importance
7. *swarming* (line 98)	g) shown clearly
8. *subservient* (line 109)	h) making a difference between
9. *emblazoned* (line 113)	i) the body without the head, arms, or legs
10. *rudimentary* (line118)	j) fighting
	k) created for the first time
	l) the state of being something new and unusual
	m) spreading out in a disordered way

Comprehension check

4 **Answer these questions.**

1. How will robot vacuum cleaners know which parts of the home need to be vacuumed?
2. Why will robot vacuum cleaners be part of some suburban homes but not all homes in 2019?
3. How will people get their personal robots to do what they want them to do?
4. Why will there be fewer people working in factories in 2019?
5. Why will factories in 2019 have smaller parking lots and fewer lunchrooms or locker rooms?
6. Why will robots need to know that human beings are in their area?

What do you think?

5 **Discuss the answers to these questions.**

1. If the author's predictions turn out to be accurate, do you think the following will have a good effect, a bad effect, or little effect on society? Why?
- Appliances linked together into intelligent work teams (paragraph 3)
- Robot vacuum cleaners (lines 43-49)
- Personal robots (lines 62-71)
2. The author states that in 2019 life will be interesting for the robot inside and outside the home. Will life be more interesting or less interesting than it is now for human beings? Why?
3. Do you think robots will ever control humans? Does such a vision of the future frighten you? Why or why not?
4. Does the text leave you with a feeling that the future as envisioned by the author is something to look forward to? Why or why not?
5. The text mentions that people may not have to do their own cooking and vacuuming in the year 2019. What other household chores would you like robots to do for you?

Vocabulary check

6 **Answer these questions.**

1. Where is the *upscale* shopping area in your town?
2. What *distinguishes* people in your part of the country from people in another part of the country?
3. Could the capital of your country be described as a *sprawling* city?
4. Have you ever experienced bees *swarming* around you?
5. Which animals usually *scurry* – dogs or mice?

Vocabulary Development 1

Prefixes and suffixes

Understanding the meaning of parts of words can help you guess the general meaning of a new word. A prefix is a group of letters added to the beginning of a word. The prefix *pre-* means "before."

> According to a *preprogrammed* schedule. . . (=the schedule would be programmed beforehand)

The prefix *micro-* means "very small."

> . . . slide out a door into the *microwave* oven.
> (=very small wavelengths)

A suffix is a group of letters added to the end of a word. The suffix *-ist* means "one who."

> *Futurists* at the Massachusetts consulting firm of Arthur D. Little . . . (=one who tries to make accurate predictions about the future)

The suffix *-ible* means "able to be."

> Those who are *visible* . . . (=able to be seen)

1 **Explain why the prefix *micro-* is part of the word for each object.**

microscope

microphone

microfilm

2 **Guess the meaning of the *italicized* words. Then answer the questions.**

1. Why is it necessary to *preheat* an oven?
2. How old are children enrolled in a *preschool* program?
3. Why is it dangerous for a baby to be born *prematurely*?
4. What is the name of a famous British or American *novelist*?
5. What rules do *motorists* in your country have to obey?
6. What kinds of activities do environmental *activists* take part in?
7. What do you do if you are reading something that is not *comprehensible*?
8. What is different about a *reversible* jacket?
9. What makes a *convertible* sofa special?

Language Focus 1

1 **Read these sentences. Then answer the questions.**

> **A.** I don't know where Sara is. She may be at home. If she's not, she may be at the supermarket.
> **B.** Alex left the office an hour ago, so he should be home by now. It never takes him more than half an hour to get home.
> **C.** Paula will be home in half an hour. Why don't you wait for her in the kitchen?

1. In which sentence does the speaker expect that the person is probably at home?
2. What word in the sentence makes it clear that this is what the speaker expects is true?

Now study the information in the Grammar Box. For further information, read Part 1 of the Language Summary on page 28.

Grammar Box 1

Form:

1. *should (not)* + base form of the verb
   ought to

Life *should be* equally interesting for the robot outside the home, especially back in the factory where it began.
Since all the machines would have at least rudimentary vision, this *should be* the simplest way of protecting human workers against death or injury.

2. *should (not)* + *be* + present participle
   ought to

By 2019, robots *ought to be doing* many things for people that people now do for themselves.

Meaning: These forms are used to express expectations, to say what you expect is true now or what you expect will be true in the future.

---

2 Rewrite the underlined part of each sentence with *should* or *ought to*.

Example:
A: Why have you decided to wait until next year to buy a new car?
B: Because I <u>expect to be making more money by then</u>.
Because I ought to be making more money by then.

1. A: Do you think the Stars will beat the Bulls?
   B: They have the better players, so <u>I expect them to win</u>.

2. A: Do we have enough chairs for the meeting?
   B: No, I think we need more. There <u>will probably be</u> more people than usual.

3. A: Well, it's 10:00. Herb's plane <u>is probably getting</u> ready to take off.
   B: Oh, how I wish I were on the plane with him.

4. A: I'll check the turkey.
   B: It <u>is probably not done</u> yet, but you can check if you want to.

5. A: I don't think I have enough money for an ice-cream cone. I have only $1.50.
   B: <u>I don't expect an ice-cream cone to cost</u> more than that.

6. A: Look how late we are.
   B: Don't worry. <u>I expect us to get</u> to the airport in plenty of time. There's hardly any traffic.

7. A: Did you read this?
   B: What?
   A: This article about life in the future. One scientist says that <u>she expects people to be living</u> in outer space 100 years from now.

3 Study the information in the Grammar Box.

Grammar Box 2

Form: *should* + *have* + past participle
        ought to
Meaning: This form is used to talk about something we expected to happen but did not happen.

According to predictions made in 1900, scientists *should have found* a way to eliminate flies and mosquitoes by now. (=People expected scientists to find a way to eliminate flies and mosquitoes by now, but scientists haven't.)

---

4 Below is a list of predictions that were made in 1900 about changes that would occur in the twentieth century. If the prediction was accurate, write *This turned out to be true.*
If the prediction was not accurate, write a sentence beginning with *According to predictions made in 1900,* then complete the sentence using *should* or *ought to*.

Examples:
People will be larger and will live longer.
This turned out to be true.

Scientists will find a way to eliminate flies and mosquitoes.
According to predictions made in 1900, scientists should have found a way to eliminate flies and mosquitoes, but they haven't.

1. Machines will be made that will keep food cool and fresh.
2. The U.S. population will grow to between 350 and 500 million. (Mexico and South American countries will join the United States to form one nation.)
3. Strawberries will become as big as apples.
4. Hydropower[1] will replace coal as a source of electricity.
5. Cars will replace horses as a means of transportation.
6. Cameras, screens, and wires will produce pictures that appear to move.
7. Engineers will develop electric-powered ships to cross the ocean in two days.
8. Inequality among people will be eliminated.

[1] hydropower: power created by water

19

5 Work with another student. Make a list of what the leaders of your country have promised to do over the past three or four years. Categorize the promises according to what has and has not been accomplished. Then tell another pair what has not been accomplished using *should* or *ought to*.

Listening

Before listening

1 Discuss the answers to these questions.

1. Central computers that regulate the temperature of each room of a home have already been developed. What other aspects of home life might computers be able to control in the future?
2. How can cars be improved?
3. What do you do when you're feeling tense and jittery[1] and you need to relax?
4. How might computers help people with their exercise programs or athletes with their training programs?

20   [1] jittery: nervous

Listening point

2 Listen to the commercials. Where would you use the products or services advertised? Choose the picture that goes with each commercial.

a

b

c

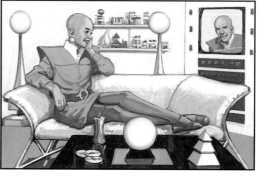

d

Comprehension check

3 Before listening to the commercials again, work with another student and try to complete the advertisements.

1. The Home Mood Sensor will take care of your every ___1___ . Wake up in the morning, and it will put the right amount of ___2___ in your coffee to get you through the day. Come home angry, and the sensor will ___3___ the room or switch on ___4___ music. Go away for a few days, and it will ___5___ doors and turn ___6___ on and off to make people believe someone is at home.

2. Perfection is a car that will never get a ___7___ . It will never have any ___8___ no matter how bad the climate is. It will never need a ___9___ . If the car has a mechanical problem, ___10___ will tell the mechanic what's wrong. If drivers get lost, the video display in the car will give ___11___ . If the car breaks down in a distant place, the car will transmit an ___12___ to a watching satellite. The car won't start if people who have had too much to ___13___ are behind the wheel. The car avoids ___14___ by braking or steering the car in the opposite direction.

3. The Purpose 1 relaxation chair is designed to relax your ___15___ and calm your mind. When you get in the chair, a light begins to ___16___ . – on...off...on...off. You start to hear ___17___ . The ___18___ of the chair move up and down in the same rhythm as your ___19___ . Then you hear the sound of ocean waves and feel a ___20___ through your hair. You can even ___21___ the water.

4. The Pro Coach computer knows how efficiently your body uses ___22___ and how powerful your ___23___ are. It uses all the information it knows about you to design a ___24___ especially for you. As you ___25___ , it lets you know how you're doing. It ___26___ you if you're overdoing it and ___27___ you if you're being lazy.

Here are the missing words. (Check with another student or your teacher to find the meaning of any new words.) How many of these words did you use to complete the ads?

arms	collisions	lights	rust	tune-up
blink	cool	microchips	scolds	voices
body	dent	muscles	slam	warns
breathing	directions	need	smell	
breeze	drink	oxygen	soothing	
caffeine	emergency call	practice	training program	

Now listen to the commercials again and check your answers.

21

What do you think?

4 Discuss the answers to these questions.

1. When do you think each item advertised will actually be for sale?
2. Which items advertised would you like for yourself? Why?
3. Do you think items like those advertised are important for the development of humanity? Or do you think it is more important for there to be less development of technology and for there to be more attention paid to solving problems like feeding and housing everyone around the world? Why?

Vocabulary check

5 Find the word which is NOT similar in meaning to the other two words.

1. bang   slam   touch
2. dent   mark   mirror
3. annoying   calming   soothing
4. accidents   collisions   highways
5. blink   flash   smile
6. laugh   scold   yell

Vocabulary Development 2

Adjectives expressing extremes

In the commercial, you heard:
Perfection is loaded with electronic options that are *astounding*
Exhausted by it all?

Astounding means "very, very surprising."
Exhausted means "very, very tired."

pretty surprising   surprising   very surprising   astounding

pretty tired   tired   very tired   exhausted

1 Match each adjective in Box A with the adjective that is stronger in degree in Box B. Use a dictionary if you need help. The first one has been done for you.

A	B
1. tired *d*	a) astounding
2. surprising	b) boiling
3. good	c) disgusting
4. bad	d) exhausted
5. dirty	e) fantastic
6. clean	f) filthy
7. pretty	g) freezing
8. funny	h) furious
9. ugly	i) gigantic
10. big	j) gorgeous
11. small	k) hideous
12. hungry	l) hilarious
13. angry	m) spotless
14. hot	n) starving
15. cold	o) tiny

2 Complete each dialogue using a word from Box B in Exercise 1.

Example:
A: Don't you think it's surprising that one day there will be cars that never get dents?
B: Surprising? I think it's *astounding*.

1. *A:* After not eating all day, you must be hungry.
   B: Hungry? I'm _____.

2. *A:* Is Mexico City a big city?
   B: Big? It's _____.

3. *A:* Are microchips small?
   B: Small? They're _____.

4. *A:* It's hot in the Sahara Desert, isn't it?
   B: Hot? It's _____.

5. *A:* Worms must taste bad.
   B: Bad? They taste _____.

6. *A:* Were you angry when the police officer made you get out of the car?
   B: Angry? I was _____.

Now work with another student. Use the remaining adjectives in Boxes A and B in Exercise 1 to make up dialogues that are similar to the dialogues in Exercise 2.

Talking Point

Work in groups of three or four students. First, think of a product or service the group would like to see developed in the future. It could be something for the home, for the school, for entertainment, or for anything else you can think of. Then make up a radio commercial to advertise this new product or service. The commercial should last from 30 to 60 seconds. Finally, record your commercial on tape or perform the commercial in front of the class.

Language Focus 2

1 Listen to the conversation and complete the sentences.

1. They still can't tell me exactly what time _____ here.
2. The representative told me _____ in the evening.
3. That's good because _____ from the teachers' conference in Dublin until midday.
4. No, that won't be any good. _____ for the conference by then.
5. No, that's no good. _____ at 9:00.

Now study the information in the Grammar Box. For further information, read Part 2 of the Language Summary on page 28.

Now study the information in the Grammar Box. For further information, read Part 2 of the Language Summary on page 28.

Grammar Box 3

1. **Form**: *will* + *be* + present participle
   I'll be teaching at 9:00.
   We'll be arriving in the evening.

Meaning: This form is used to talk about:
a) activities that will be in progress at a specific time in the future.
b) events that will happen as a matter of course.

2. **Form**: *will* + *have* + past participle
   I'll have left for the conference by then.

Meaning: This form is used to talk about an action that will be finished or a state that will be reached before a certain time in the future.

---

2 Complete these sentences with *will* and the correct form of the verbs.

1. *A:* What _____ (you/do) this time next year?
   B: Who knows?

2. *A:* Have you been married long?
   B: This April 7 we _____ (be married) twenty wonderful years.

3. *A:* Should we come at 2:00?
   B: No, I _____ (probably wash) clothes. Why don't you come a little later?
   A: Okay. Then we _____ (come) at 3:00.

4. *A:* I don't think I'll be able to get to the movie theater until 8:30.
   B: But the movie _____ (already start). The paper says it starts at 8:15.

5. *A:* The class is having a party tomorrow night. Would you like to come? I'm sure you _____ (have) a good time.
   B: I'd love to, but I can't. I _____ (correct) your test papers, and I doubt I _____ (have) as good a time as you.

6. *A:* When will you be able to give me back my essay?
   B: On Friday. _____ (have) a chance to look at it by then.

3 Decide with another student what your teacher's probable activities will be tomorrow at the following times:

5:00 A.M.   11:00 A.M.   1:30 P.M.   4:00 P.M.   6:30 P.M.
9:00 P.M.   11:30 P.M.

   Example: *At 5:00 A.M., she'll be getting ready to go to work.*

Now confirm your predictions by asking your teacher questions.

   Example: *Will you be getting ready to go to work at 5:00 A.M.?*

4 Look at the headlines. Which ones do you think will be true by the year 2050? Make sentences with *will*. (Note: Use the passive and add *a* or *the* where necessary.)

   Example:

I'm sure
I think   } that by 2050 robots will have taken
I doubt   over all factory work.

1. **ROBOTS TAKE OVER ALL FACTORY**

2. **OIL RUNS OUT**

3. **WOMAN ELECTED PRESIDENT OF THE U.S.**

4. **ELEPHANTS BECOME EXTINCT**

5. **SCIENTISTS FIND CURE FOR CANCER**

6. **ALL NUCLEAR WEAPONS DESTROYED**

7. **U.S.A. SEPARATES INTO THREE COUNTRIES**

8. **WATER SHORTAGE BECOMES SERIOUS GLOBAL PROBLEM**

5 Work with another student. Answer each question with a different name. Decide who in your class is:

1. the most ambitious
2. the most inventive
3. the most artistic
4. the most adventurous
5. most likely to succeed
6. most likely to have a lot of children
7. most likely to become rich
8. most likely to become famous
9. most likely to become a fashion model
10. most likely to become a workaholic

Decide with your partner what the lives of these people will be like in 10 years. Think of as many things as you can. When you finish, tell these people your predictions.

Example:
Pablo is the most ambitious in the class. In 10 years he'll probably be running a big company. He'll be making a lot of money. He'll have bought two homes and four cars. He'll be considering getting involved in politics.

Writing

A. Subject-verb agreement

1 The writing section in Unit 2, Book A contained six rules about subject-verb agreement. This section contains six more. Read the rules. Check (✓) the rules which are NOT new to you.

1. A singular verb is used with the following words when they are used as subjects:

everyone	someone	anyone	no one	each
everybody	somebody	anybody	nobody	either
everything	something	anything	nothing	neither

    S   V
<u>Everyone</u> <u>hopes</u> for a bright future.

    S
<u>Nobody</u>, not even the most well-known futurists,

  V
<u>knows</u> exactly what the future will be like.

2. A singular verb is used when the subject is the title of a written work, a movie, or a business company even if the title is plural in form.

          S   V
<u>The Future and The Past</u> <u>is</u> a book that compares life 100 years from now and life 100 years ago.

3. A singular verb is used with subjects that state an amount (for example, of money, time, or distance).

              S   V
<u>Seventy thousand dollars</u> <u>is</u> how much the average car will cost in 2019.

4. A singular verb is usually used with subjects that are plural in form but singular in meaning.
Subjects: *mathematics*, *physics*, etc.
Abstract nouns: *news*, *politics*, etc.

  S   V   V
<u>Physics</u> <u>has played</u> and <u>will continue</u> to play an important role in the development of modern technology.

5. A singular verb is usually used with collective nouns (*group*, *family*, *team*, *police*, *committee*, and *class*). However, if the speaker is thinking more in terms of the individuals that make up the group, a plural verb is used.

           S   V
The <u>committee</u> <u>is looking</u> into how to prevent the spread of the disease.

           S   V
The <u>committee</u> <u>are meeting</u> today. (=The members of the committee are meeting today.)
I saw them enter the room a short time ago.

6. A singular verb is used with *the number of*. A plural verb is used with *a number of*.

           S
The <u>number</u> of people who want to travel in

            V
outer space <u>is</u> amazing.

       S   V
A <u>number</u> of studies <u>are looking</u> into ways robots can improve our quality of life.

2 Underline the subject in each sentence. Then choose the correct verb form to complete the sentence.

1. Everybody (hope, hopes) there will be no more wars.
2. Nothing (has, have) been completely successful yet in stopping the spread of the deadly disease.
3. *War and Peace* (was, were) written by Leo Tolstoy.
4. H.M. Vehicles (publish, publishes) a booklet about cars that are not much bigger than motor-cycles.
5. One hundred and fifty kilometers (is, are) a long distance to go on just three liters of gasoline, but in the future it may be possible.
6. The news (is, are) good: By 2019, world hunger should be eliminated.
7. The class (has, have) completed more than half of the book.
8. There (is, are) a number of engineers who think that one day it will be possible to travel from New York to Los Angeles in just 21 minutes.
9. The number of robots in factories (is, are) growing every year.

B. Outlining

Before you begin to write an essay, it is helpful to outline your ideas. In this way, you can think in advance of the main points you want to make and the details you are going to use to support your main points.

1 Use the information below to complete the outline for a five-paragraph essay entitled "Unusual Tasks for Robots." Identify the main idea for each of the middle paragraphs, and then choose the three supporting details that support each main idea.

- analyze soil and fertilize it when necessary
- decide when a plant is ripe for picking
- guide a blind person on the street
- hand things to a person in a wheelchair
- help in dangerous situations
- help on the farm
- help paralyzed people learn to walk again
- help the handicapped
- help the police defuse terrorist bombs
- inspect the interior of a nuclear reactor
- locate weeds and kill them
- search for survivors inside a burning building

I.   Introduction
II. Main idea one: _____
     Supporting details:
     A. _____
     B. _____
     C. _____
III. Main idea two: _____
     Supporting details:
     A. _____
     B. _____
     C. _____
IV. Main idea three: _____
     Supporting details:
     A. _____
     B. _____
     C. _____
V.   Conclusion

2 People put objects in time capsules and then bury them so that when people in later generations open these containers, they will have an idea what life was like in earlier times. Imagine you were asked to contribute an essay entitled "Life in Our Times" to a time capsule. What type of information would you include to give the people who find the capsule in later generations the clearest picture of life nowadays? How would you organize your ideas? Prepare an outline for this essay with one or two other students. When you finish, compare outlines with other groups.

3 Write an essay using the outline you wrote in Exercise 2, or write an outline for one of these topics and develop it into an essay.

1. My Ideal Future
2. The National Agenda: What Our Leaders Should Work to Change in the Next 20 Years
3. Who Controls Your Future: You or Fate?
4. How Having Your Fortune Told Can Change Your Life

Language Summary

Part 1: Expressing expectations

Present / future time

1. Form: *should (not)* + base form of the verb
　　　ought to
Life *should be* equally interesting for the robot outside the home, especially back in the factory where it began.
Since all the machines would have at least rudimentary vision, this *should be* the simplest way of protecting human workers against death or injury.

2. Form: *should (not)* + *be* + present participle
　　　ought to
By 2019, robots *ought to be doing* many things for people that people now do for themselves.

Meaning: These forms are used to express expectations, to say what you expect is true now or what you expect will be true in the future.

Past time

Form: *should* + *have* + past participle
　　　ought to
According to predictions made in 1900, scientists *should have found* a way to eliminate flies and mosquitoes by now.
(=People expected scientists to find a way by now, but scientists haven't.)

Meaning: This form is used to talk about something we expected to happen but did not happen.

Point to remember: *Should* and *ought to* are similar in meaning, but *ought to* is less common and is rarely used in negative form.

Part 2: Talking about the future

Future progressive

Form: *will* + *be* + present participle
We'll *be arriving* in the evening.

Meaning:
a) This form is used to talk about an activity that will be in progress at a specific time in the future.
I *will be teaching* at 9:00. (=I will begin teaching before 9:00 and continue after 9:00.)

b) This form is also used to talk about events that will happen as a matter of course, i.e., events that happen naturally: nobody has made any plans, decisions, or promises; things just happen this way.
We'll *be discussing* different topics at the conference.
(=That is what normally happens at a conference.)

Points to remember:
a) It is also possible to use *be going to.*
We're *going to be arriving* in the evening.

b) Sometimes there is little or no difference between the future progressive and the simple future, especially when the future time is not specified.
We'll *eat* soon.
We'll *be eating* soon.

Future perfect

Form: *will* + *have* + past participle
I *will have left* for the conference by then.

Meaning: This form is used to talk about an action that will be finished or a state that will be reached before a certain time in the future.
By the end of this course, we'll *have finished* this book.
(=It is not known exactly when we will finish it, but it will be sometime before the end of this course.)

u n i t
three

ALL WORK AND NO PLAY MAKE JACK A DULL BOY

Talking Point

How much do you agree with each of the following statements? There are five possible answers:
Strongly Agree (1),   Agree (2),   Neutral (3),
Disagree (4),   Strongly Disagree (5).
Circle the appropriate number.

1. People are spending too much time at work nowadays, to the detriment of their homes, their families, their personal lives, and their communities.

   1   2   3   4   5

2. A modern society cannot have a thriving economy if its workers work 3 to 4 hours a day, 15 to 20 hours a week.

   1   2   3   4   5

3. People who work long hours have a higher standard of living than people who work shorter hours.

   1   2   3   4   5

4. Advances in technology, such as computers and fax machines, allow people to have more leisure time.

   1   2   3   4   5

5. A 40-hour workweek, 8 hours a day, 5 days a week, 50 weeks a year is a reasonable amount of time for people to work.

   1   2   3   4   5

6. People's work is the most important thing in their life.

   1   2   3   4   5

7. People who do not work long and hard are lazy, unproductive, and worthless.

   1   2   3   4   5

8. Leisure-time activities – such as play, relaxation, engaging in cultural and artistic pursuits, or just contemplation and "doing nothing" – are not essential or worthwhile components of life.

   1   2   3   4   5

Now compare answers with other students. Be sure to give the reasons for your choices.

Reading

Before reading

1 The reading you are going to read is entitled "Less Is More: A Call for Shorter Work Hours." The first sentence in the reading is "America is suffering from overwork." Check (✓) the four subjects below that you think will be discussed in the article.

1. How much people in other countries work
2. Why it is difficult to get Americans to work less
3. Why students should decide on their career before they graduate from high school
4. Why overwork can be bad for people
5. Why work is so important to Americans
6. What people should do to find a good job

Less Is More: A Call for Shorter Work Hours

America is suffering from overwork. Too many of us are too busy, trying to squeeze more into each day while having less
5 **to show for it. Although our growing time crunch is often portrayed as a personal dilemma, it is in fact a major social problem that has reached**
10 **crisis proportions over the past 20 years.**

The simple fact is that Americans today—both women and men—are spending too much time at work, to
15 the detriment of their homes, their families, their personal lives, and their communities. The American Dream promised that our individual hard work paired with the advances
20 of modern technology would bring about the good life for all. Glorious visions of the leisure society were touted[1] throughout the '50s and '60s. However, most people are now
25 working more than ever before, while still struggling to meet their economic commitments. Ironically, the many advances in technology, such as computers and fax machines,
30 rather than reducing our workload, seem to have speeded up our lives at work. At the same time, technology has equipped us with "conveniences" like microwave ovens and frozen
35 dinners that merely enable us to adopt a similar frantic pace in our home lives so we can cope with more hours at paid work. [. . .]

Americans often assume that
40 overwork is an inevitable fact of life—like death and taxes. Yet a closer look at other times and other nations offers some startling surprises.

45 Anthropologists have observed that in pre-industrial (particularly hunting and gathering) societies, people generally spend 3 to 4 hours a day, 15 to 20 hours a week, doing
50 the work necessary to maintain life. The rest of the time is spent in socializing, partying, playing, storytelling, and artistic or religious activities. The ancient Romans
55 celebrated 175 public festivals a year in which everyone participated, and people in the Middle Ages had at least 115.

In our era, almost every other
60 industrialized nation (except Japan) has fewer annual working hours and longer vacations than the United States. This includes all of Western Europe, where many nations enjoy
65 thriving economies and standards of living equal to or higher than ours. [. . .]

While the idea of a shorter workweek and longer vacations
70 sounds appealing to most people, any movement to enact shorter work-time as a public policy will encounter surprising pockets of resistance, not just from business
75 leaders but even from some workers. Perhaps the most formidable barrier to more free time for Americans is the widespread mind-set[2] that the 40-hour workweek, 8 hours a day,
80 5 days a week, 50 weeks a year, is a natural rhythm of the universe.

A second obstacle to launching shorter work-time is America's deeply ingrained work ethic[3]. This
85 work ethic fosters the widely held belief that people's work is their most important activity and that people who do not work long and hard are lazy, unproductive, and
90 worthless.

For many Americans today, paid work is not just a way to make money but is a crucial source of their self-worth. Many of us identify
95 ourselves almost entirely by the kind of work we do. Work still has a powerful psychological and spiritual hold over our lives—and talk of shorter work-time may seem
100 somehow morally suspicious.

Because we are so deeply a work-oriented society, leisure-time activities —such as play, relaxation, engaging in cultural and artistic pursuits, or just
105 quiet contemplation and "doing nothing"—are not looked on as essential and worthwhile components of life.

Of course, the stiffest opposition to
110 cutting work hours comes not from citizens but from business. Employers are reluctant to alter the 8-hour day, 40-hour workweek, 50 weeks a year because it seems easier and more
115 profitable for employers to hire fewer employees for longer hours rather than more employees—each of whom would also require health insurance and other benefits—with flexible
120 schedules and work arrangements. [. . .]

Our role as consumers also contributes to keeping the average workweek from falling. In an economic system in which addictive
125 buying is the basis of corporate profits, working a full 40 hours or more each week for 50 weeks a year gives us just enough time to stumble home and

dazedly[4]—almost automatically—
130 shop; but not enough time to think about deeper issues or to work effectively for social change. From the point of view of corporations and policymakers, shorter work-time may
135 be bad for the economy, because people with enhanced[5] free time may begin to find other things to do with it besides mindlessly buying products. It takes more free time to grow
140 vegetables, cook meals from scratch, sew clothes, or repair broken items than it does to just buy these things at the mall.

[1] touted: described as being something wonderful
[2] mind-set: a fixed attitude or state of mind
[3] work ethic: the belief that work is morally good
[4] dazedly: unable to think or feel clearly
[5] enhanced: increased

Guessing meaning

3 Match each word in Column A with its meaning in Column B. (Note: Be careful. There are three extra choices in Column B.)

A	B
1. *dilemma* (line 8)	a) unavoidable
2. *ironically* (line 27)	b) an easy decision
3. *frantic* (line 36)	c) not really wanting to do something
4. *inevitable* (line 40)	
5. *enact* (line 71)	d) using food already prepared and sold in containers
6. *formidable* (line 76)	
7. *launch* (line 82)	e) using basic ingredients
8. *foster* (line 85)	f) make into law
9. *reluctant* (line 112)	g) a difficult situation for which there does not seem to be a satisfactory solution
10. *from scratch* (line 140)	
	h) encourage
	i) not surprisingly
	j) difficult
	k) having the opposite result from what is expected
	l) put into action
	m) fast and nervous

4 What do these words mean?

1. *commitment* (line 27)
2. *appealing* (line 70)
3. *barrier* (line 76)
4. *deeply ingrained* (line 84)
5. *stiffest* (line 109)

Comprehension check

5 Check (✓) the statements with which the authors of the article would probably agree. Write down the parts of the text that show they would probably agree.

Example: Americans are working too much.

Line(s) *1 and 2*

1. Women should stop working outside the home.

Line(s) _____

2. The American family is suffering because of the hours parents spend away from their children.

Line(s) _____

3. People who are now in their 30s and 40s have an easier life than their parents did.   Line(s) _____

4. Americans should work less than 40 hours a week, 50 weeks a year.   Line(s) _____

5. Americans should learn that there are other things in life as important as or more important than one's work.   Line(s) _____

6. Americans should learn to relax.   Line(s) _____

7. Americans should not make buying things a central part of their lives.   Line(s) _____

8. American workers should demand more money from their employers so that they can work fewer hours.   Line(s) _____

What do you think?

6 Discuss the answers to these questions.

1. What does "trying to squeeze more into each day while having less to show for it" (lines 3 to 5) mean?
2. Is the work ethic deeply ingrained in your society? Why is the work ethic deeply ingrained in certain societies but less important in other societies?
3. What is the average amount of time a working person in your country spends at work, with the family, and alone pursuing leisure activities? Do you think more or less time should be devoted to any one area? Why?
4. Who has had a healthier, more satisfying working life—working people nowadays or people of your grandparents' generation? Why?
5. Has the fact that people nowadays are able to buy more material things improved their quality of life? Why or why not?
6. Which is worse—people who try to work as little as possible and own few material things or people who work 60 to 70 hours a week so that their family has all that it needs? Why?

31

Vocabulary check

7 Answer these questions.

1. If you had a *dilemma,* who would you talk to to help you decide what to do?
2. Who has more *commitments* – a single person or a married person? Give examples.
3. What may happen to a person who leads a *frantic* lifestyle for a long time?
4. Would you think a job offer was *appealing* if the director of the company promised you a very good salary for working 55 hours a week?
5. Would you be *reluctant* to lend a friend a lot of money if you knew he or she could not pay you back for a long time?

Language Focus 1

1 Combine each phrase in the box with an appropriate sentence to make new sentences. (Note: Be sure to use the correct punctuation.)

> a few of which I still do not understand
> most of whom had at least one question
> none of whose names are known

1. Several people were involved in writing the article on page 30.
2. The article on page 30 had many new words.
3. My classmates asked the teacher for help.

Now study the information in the Grammar Box. For further information, read Part 1 of the Language Summary on page 42.

Grammar Box 1

The *italicized* part in this sentence is an example of a relative clause with an expression of quantity.

It seems easier for employers to hire fewer employees for longer hours rather than more employees, *each of whom would also receive health insurance and other benefits.*

---

2 Combine the sentences with a relative clause.

Example:
These couples often talk about what they think of as the "good old days." Few of these couples' parents ever worked so much.
These couples, few of whose parents ever worked so much, often talk about what they think of as the "good old days."

1. I'm interested in this subject and have read several articles. Two of these articles have reached the same conclusions.
2. Many parents say they are working long hours for the family. Few of these parents have much free time to spend with their children.
3. These parents feel guilty if they are not able to give their children whatever they desire. Some of these parents grew up with almost nothing.
4. My group discussed the problem with a psychiatrist. One of the psychiatrist's biggest concerns is the effect this has on children.
5. He has spoken at parents' meetings. Several of these meetings have taken place at the local high school.

3 Rewrite each sentence and include a relative clause that has an expression of quantity.

Example: On the street there are other buildings.
On the street there are other buildings, one of which looks exactly like this one.

1. There are many students in this class.
2. I have several English books.
3. It is difficult to master English grammar.
4. Many teachers have tried to help me with this problem.
5. It is sometimes difficult to understand English speakers.

Vocabulary Development 1

Prefixes

A prefix is a group of letters added to the beginning of a word. The prefix *over-* means "too much."

America is suffering from *overwork*.
(=too much work)

The prefix *self-* means "of or by oneself."

. . . paid work is a crucial source of people's *self-worth*. (=people's opinion of their value in society)

The prefix *under-* means "less than it should be."

. . . people who feel they are *underpaid*.
(=paid less than they should be paid)

1 Read the sentences and choose the meaning of the *italicized* words.

1. When she speaks in front of a group, she's very *self-conscious*.
   a) nervous and concerned about what others will think of her
   b) nervous and concerned that she won't like what others do

2. Whatever he does, he does out of *self-interest*.
   a) concern for what is best for others
   b) concern for what is best for him

3. I think you've *oversimplified* the problem.
   a) made the problem seem more simple than it is
   b) made the problem seem more complex than it is

4. We *overestimated* how much it would cost to fix your car, so you need to write a check for only $150, not $200.
   a) thought it would cost more than it did
   b) thought it would cost less than it did

5. This chicken is *undercooked*. You'd better put it back in the oven.
   a) cooked less than it should be cooked
   b) cooked more than it should be cooked

6. To reduce the population in our cities, we would like to encourage people to move to *underpopulated* areas of the country.
   a) having more people than normal
   b) having fewer people than normal

7. All the middle-class people I know are angry because they're *overextended* with mortgage payments, car payments, and credit card debt.
   a) in financial difficulty because they have spent more money than they have
   b) in no financial difficulty because they have not spent much money

2 Complete these sentences by adding *over*, *self-*, or *under*.

Example: This gas station is *self*-service. You have to pump your own gas.

1. It may surprise people to learn that such a successful man is completely __taught__. He never went to school.
2. You need to be __confident__. If you don't think you will be able to do it, you won't be able to.
3. These vegetables are __cooked__. They're soft and tasteless.
4. Excuse me, I think you __charged__ me. I paid $19.95, but the sign says this shirt costs $16.95.
5. There are many children around the world who are __nourished__. Because they do not get enough to eat, they are not as healthy as they should be.
6. I'm afraid, Ms. Gomez, that you are __qualified__ for this job. We're looking for someone with less education and less experience than you have.
7. I think you've __rated__ her abilities. She's much more capable than you had told me she was.
8. You need to have __control__ in order to lose weight. Every time you want to eat some chocolate, you have to be able to tell yourself "No."
9. Put the baby to bed. She's crying so much because she's __tired__.
10. When I __eat__, I feel sick to my stomach.
11. My father's __employed__. The store he owns is called Currans.

33

Language Focus 2

1 Read these two sentences. Then answer the questions.

   A. While living in Atlanta, Bill had two full-time jobs.

   B. While he was living in Atlanta, Bill had two full-time jobs.

   1. Do sentences **A** and **B** have the same meaning or a different meaning?
   2. Does *while* express time or contrast?
   3. What has been omitted in sentence **A**?
   4. What is the subject of *while living in Atlanta*?
   5. What is the subject of the main clause—*Bill had two full-time jobs*?

Now study the information in the Grammar Box. For further information, read Part 2 of the Language Summary on page 42.

Grammar Box 2

In an adverb clause of time, the subject and the *be* form of the verb can be omitted if the subject of the adverb clause and the main clause is the same. Look at this sentence from the reading. The *italicized* part is an example of a reduced adverb clause.

> Most people are now working more than ever before, *while still struggling to meet their economic commitments.* (=while they are still struggling to meet their economic commitments)

---

2 Change the adverb clause in each sentence to a reduced adverb clause if possible.

   Example:
   Since I met Jackie, I've heard a lot of strange stories.
   Since meeting Jackie, I've heard a lot of strange stories.

   1. Before Jackie became a private investigator, she had had many kinds of jobs.
   2. Jackie decided that this was the job for her while she was working as a reporter for a small-town paper.
   3. After Jackie became an investigator, a police officer told her that women investigators have an advantage because "nobody ever expects them to be getting information."
   4. She has had many interesting cases since she opened her office.
   5. Before she became well-known, she charged only $15 an hour.
   6. But she has been charging $85 an hour since she solved a case that was written about in all the local papers.
   7. However, before others decide they want to be investigators, Jackie suggests they find out what the job is really like.

3 Complete each sentence truthfully with a reduced adverb clause. Read your sentences to another student and give more details.

   Example:
   I met an interesting person the other day *while standing in line at the bank. He told me about his recent travels in India. I enjoyed talking to him so much that we agreed to meet again.*

   1. I made a mistake . . .
   2. I saw something strange . . .
   3. I made a decision about what to do . . .
   4. I became worried one day . . .
   5. I couldn't stop laughing . . .
   6. I got very angry . . .

Talking Point

There are six types of people listed in the box. Each type of person is described in paragraphs a) to f) below. Read each description and match each type in the box with the description. (Check with another student or your teacher to find the meaning of any new words.) Then decide which type you are.

A
Type
1. practical   4. outgoing
2. intellectual   5. persuasive
3. creative   6. adaptive

**B
Description**

a) These people prefer highly structured[1] verbal and numerical activities. They seem to work best in well-established chains of command[2]. They tend to value material possessions and status more than physical skills or personal relationships.

b) These people are usually sociable, responsible, humanistic, and caring people. They tend to express themselves well and prefer to solve problems through discussion or by working with people on an interpersonal level. They often like to be the center of attention or to be near the center of activity.

c) These people are strong, aggressive, and physically skillful. They usually prefer working with objects and things more than with people and ideas. They may have difficulty putting their feelings into words.

d) These people are original, creative, and task-oriented[3]. They usually enjoy solving abstract problems and working to understand the physical world. They often have unconventional values[4] and attitudes and prefer unstructured settings with freedom to think problems through.

e) These people are often sensitive, emotional, unconventional in outlook, and have a great need for self-expression. They may be reluctant to assert[5] their opinions or capabilities except through their art.

f) These people are usually energetic, enthusiastic, self-confident, and enjoy persuading others to their viewpoints. They often prefer power, status, and material wealth to precise, long-term intellectual effort.

Now work in groups and decide which of these jobs are suitable for which types of people. (Note: There are two jobs for each type.) Then decide on other jobs which would be suitable for each type of person. When you finish, compare answers with someone from another group.

accountant

airplane pilot

air traffic controller

banker

child-care worker

engineer

fire fighter

interior designer

journalist

politician

salesperson

typist

[1] highly structured: highly organized
[2] well-established chains of command: situations where a person waits to be told what to do before doing a task
[3] task-oriented: (of people) who set goals for a specific task and achieve their goals
[4] unconventional values: different from the usual values of a society
[5] assert: express forcefully

Listening

Before listening

1 Write the words in the correct column. Write any words that were common 35 years ago AND are still common in both columns.

> answering machine
> black and white television
> computer
> credit card debt
> date book
> fax machine
> mortgage payment
> phone with rotary dial

COMMON 35 YEARS AGO	COMMON NOWADAYS

date book

phone with a rotary dial

Listening point

2 You will hear a journalist who works for National Public Radio speak about her life. First listen to the introduction. Then write down what you think the talk will be about.

Now listen to the talk. Did you predict the subject of the talk?

Comprehension check

3 Listen to the tape again. Does each of these descriptions relate to *35 years ago* or *nowadays*?

1. time for dinners
2. a lot of stuff in people's homes
3. people angry because of all their debt
4. slow, reflective time disappearing
5. long, slow talks at college
6. college students busy all the time
7. children pushed from activity to activity
8. long summer days spent wandering

Making inferences

4 Answer these questions.

1. Why did East Germans suddenly have no time for their friends?
2. What is wrong with consuming too much?
3. What is wrong with pushing children from activity to activity?
4. Why would parents who live in unsafe areas be glad if the school year were made longer?
5. Why does the speaker wish she had weekly newspapers instead of daily newspapers?

What do you think?

5 **Discuss the answers to these questions.**

1. What did the speaker mention that was also mentioned in the text on page 30?
2. Are there people in your society who might feel the same way as the speaker?
3. What are the good and bad points of children being pushed from activity to activity?
4. Do people of your generation consume more than your grandparents did when they were young? What effects has this had on your society?
5. If the speaker came to live in your country, would she find the lifestyle she would like to have? Give examples.
6. What advice would you give to people like the speaker, who feel they never have enough time to do what they want?

Vocabulary check

6 **The speaker used the *italicized* words. If you cannot remember the context in which they were used, check the tapescript. Then answer the questions.**

1. Are your country's economic problems slightly worse, *drastically* worse, or not worse than they were ten years ago?
2. If you were *in debt,* how would you solve your problem?
3. Do you have an *abundance* of free time?
4. If you weren't able to meet a *deadline,* would you lie about why you couldn't do it or would you admit the truth?
5. Is there anything you *long for*?

Language Focus 3

1 **Listen to the tape.**
Then answer these questions.

1. Where is the woman?
2. What is the problem?

Now listen to the tape again and complete these sentences.

1. I _____ in my briefcase.
2. I _____ at home.
3. He _____ the children to school.

Now study the information in the Grammar Box. For further information, read Part 3 of the Language Summary on page 42.

Grammar Box 3

1. **Form:** *must (not)* + base form of the verb
The papers *must be* at home. (=I'm almost sure, but not completely sure, that the papers are at home.)

Meaning: This form is used to express a strong degree of certainty about a present situation or action.

2. **Form:** *must (not)* + *be* + present participle
He *must be taking* the children to school. (=I'm almost sure, but not completely sure, that he's taking the children to school.)

Meaning: This form is used to express a strong degree of certainty about an action in progress at the time of speaking.

3. **Form:** *must (not)* + *have* + past participle
I *must have put* the report in my briefcase. (=I'm almost sure, but not completely sure, that I put the report in my briefcase.)

Meaning: This form is used to express a strong degree of certainty about an action or situation that happened in the past.

2 Complete the sentences by using *must* and one of the phrases in the box. Be sure to put the verb in the correct form.

be an emergency	be married	be really angry
be rich	like animals	look for something
oversleep	sleep	speed	take a shower

Examples:
Murray has four cats and a dog.
He *must like animals.*
Patty refused to talk to me for two weeks.
She *must have been really angry.*

1. Where's David? He's already 15 minutes late. He _____
2. When Ted Thompson died, his daughter inherited his Rolls Royce, his Mercedes, his ten homes, and his two yachts. He _____
3. Alice's bedroom door is shut, and all the lights are out. She _____
4. I _____ when you called last night. I never hear the phone when I'm in the bathroom.
5. Tom's on his hands and knees. He _____
6. Why was the doctor at the hospital so late last night? There _____
7. The teacher is wearing a wedding ring. She _____
8. The police officer is giving the driver a ticket. He _____

3 Complete this conversation with the correct form of *must* or *have to* and the verbs in parentheses. Add *not* where necessary.

Kay: Why's your husband home all the time these days?

Mia: He quit his job at the hotel about a month ago.

Kay: You __1__ (be) upset when he came home and told you that.

Mia: Not at all. I was glad he quit. When he was working there, he was never home. He always __2__ (work) overtime.

Kay: __3__ (he/work) on weekends, too?

Mia: Not always but often enough to ruin our social life. He was working 70 hours a week. The only good thing was that he __4__ (work) on holidays. He __5__ (drive) too far, either. It only took him 20 minutes to get to the hotel from here.

Kay: Working such long hours __6__ (be) very tiring.

Mia: You can say that again. It was terrible. As soon as he would come home, he'd go straight to bed. I __7__ (take care) of the children and the house all by myself.

Kay: What made him finally quit?

Mia: One day the director told him he __8__ (do) a report all over again because he had done it the wrong way.

Kay: That __9__ (please) him.

Mia: It wasn't that. When my husband said that he had done it exactly the way the director had told him to, the director told my husband he __10__ (misunderstand). He said he would have never told anyone to write a report in such an unprofessional manner. My husband got so angry that he quit that very moment.

4 Work with another student. What logical deductions can you make from the statements? Who was speaking to whom? Where were they? What was the reason for making the statement? Use *may, might,* or *must,* according to how certain you are. When you finish, tell a student from another pair what your deductions were.

1. You never catch any fish.
2. Take my picture.
3. Drop your gun!
4. This examination is impossible.
5. You are not permitted to cross the border.
6. Help me into my dress.
7. That makes 144.
8. Let's have some coffee.
9. Pass me the lemons.
10. I'm not particularly fond of snakes.

Vocabulary Development 2

Suffixes

A suffix is a group of letters added to the end of a word. There are certain suffixes used to change a verb into a noun. For example, verbs ending in *-sume* are changed into nouns by dropping the *e* and adding *-ption.*

> People *consume* a lot.
> There is a lot of *consumption.*

1 Look at the nouns and verbs in each box. Then fill in the missing nouns. What spelling change is necessary when each suffix is added to the verb?

Verb	Noun
consume	consumption
assume	1. _____
resume	2. _____
presume	3. _____

Verb	Noun
realize	realization
socialize	socialization
memorize	4. _____
generalize	5. _____

Verb	Noun
celebrate	celebration
participate	participation
investigate	6. _____
donate	7. _____

Verb	Noun
unify	unification
qualify	qualification
notify	8. _____

Now use a dictionary to check the pronunciation of the verbs and nouns. Then check (✓) the correct columns.

Verb suffix	Noun suffix	Change in pronunciation of vowels	No change in pronunciation of vowels
1. -sume	-ption		
2. -ize	-ation		
3. -ate	-ion		
4. -ify	-cation		

2 There are exceptions to the verb-noun patterns in Exercise 1. Circle the verb in each group which does NOT follow the pattern. Use a dictionary if you need help.

Example: specialize (criticize) organize
(The noun of *criticize* is *criticism.*)

1. symbolize   modernize   legalize
2. justify   satisfy   identify
3. equalize   centralize   italicize
4. characterize   individualize   recognize
5. debate   discriminate   create
6. verify   terrify   simplify

Writing

A. Linking words

Linking words connect the ideas between two sentences. They make clear the connection between what we are going to say and what came before. For example, the use of *however* below shows that there is a contrast between the first and second sentence. The first sentence is positive in meaning; the second is negative.

> Glorious visions of the leisure society were touted throughout the '50s and '60s. *However*, most people are now working more than ever before, while still struggling to meet their economic commitments.

Although there are several linking words to show contrast, they cannot all be used in place of one another.

However / On the other hand

These are used to give the other side of the story, to say, "Yes, but it is also true that . . . ."
> The job is not very interesting. *On the other hand*, it pays well.

> Jack Perkins is a hard worker. However, his brother is lazy.

However / Nevertheless

These are used to state an unexpected result, to say, "It is surprising but it is true that . . . ."
> The job is not very interesting. *Nevertheless*, I'm not going to quit.

> Jack Perkins is a hard worker. *However*, his manager is always complaining.

On the contrary

This is used to contradict, to say that the opposite is true.
> *A:* The job must not have been very interesting.
>
> *B:* On the contrary, I thought it was fascinating.

On the contrary is also used to emphasize the speaker's own negative statement by restating it in the affirmative. In this way, the speaker contradicts what he or she thinks someone else believes.
> People don't work less than they used to. *On the contrary*, they work more.

Remember that a period, NOT a comma, is used at the end of the first sentence. The linking word usually comes at the beginning of the next sentence and is followed by a comma. If the linking word comes after the subject, a comma is used before and after the linking word.

> Glorious visions of the leisure society were touted throughout the '50s and '60s. Most people, however, are now working more than ever before, while still struggling to meet their economic commitments.

1 Choose the correct linking word to complete each sentence.

1. Teaching is not always a well-paying job. (However/On the contrary), it can be one of the lower-paying jobs in society.
2. Being a doctor requires many years of training. (Nevertheless/On the other hand), many young people want to go to medical school.
3. You have the right qualifications for the job. (On the other hand/Nevertheless), I'm afraid we're unable to offer you the job.
4. She has the right experience for the job. (On the contrary/On the other hand), she does not have the education we would like someone in this position to have.
5. Ray has been looking for a job for almost half a year. (On the contrary/Nevertheless), he has been unable to find anything.
6. The government had several plans to reduce unemployment. (However/On the contrary), nothing has been done.
7. No previous training is required for the job. (However/On the contrary), we prefer someone who we can train ourselves.

2 Complete each sentence logically.

1. I try to speak English whenever I can. Nevertheless, . . .
2. There are people who study English for many years. However, . . .
3. Some people know only their native language. On the other hand, . . .
4. Learning English grammar is not easy. On the contrary, . . .
5. Many people think that English is not as romantic a language as French. Nevertheless, . . .
6. I didn't know there was a difference in meaning between all these contrast words. On the contrary, . . .

B. Introductory paragraphs

A well-written essay begins with an introductory paragraph that convinces the reader that the essay is worth reading. An effective introductory paragraph:

- states the topic of the essay.
- captures the reader's interest.
- is an integral part of the essay, not a paragraph that is just added on.

1 **Read this outline for a composition entitled "Retirement Is Not Always What People Expect It to Be."**

    I. Introductory paragraph
    II. Main idea one: Boredom
        A. Sleep a lot
        B. Watch TV a lot
        C. Complain a lot
    III. Main idea two: Questioning of one's self-worth
        A. Sense of no longer being "somebody"
        B. Sense of being useless
        C. Sense of being unwanted by society
    IV. Main idea three: Sense of being old
        A. Worried about health
        B. Concerned about being left alone
        C. Anxious about dying
    V. Concluding paragraph

Now read four different introductory paragraphs for the essay. Then answer the questions.

a) Len was a man who, from the age of 55 to his last day of employment shortly after his 65th birthday, spoke of almost nothing else but what he was going to do when he retired. Every day was the same: "I can't wait until the day I turn 65. From then on, my life will be carefree, without a worry in the world. I will be free to do all that I have dreamt of doing." When that day finally came, what happened to all of Len's plans and expectations? He sat home all day long, day in and day out, worried about money and generally making himself miserable. It was only when he opened a small store at the age of 67 and was working from nine to five, five days a week that he found happiness and felt like himself again. Len is just one of many who have learned that retirement is not what they had expected it to be, nor what they want in life.

b) People spend much of their working lives looking forward to retirement, yet when they reach their "golden years," many have a sense of being lost. Boredom seems to take over their lives with one day seeming very much like the next. They no longer have a sense of who they are, and when they look at themselves in the mirror, they suddenly see nothing but an old face. Because of this disappointment with retired life, many senior citizens actually long for the days when they were part of the working world.

c) In this essay I am going to talk about what happens to people when they retire. While it is true that there are people who enjoy being retired, there are many who find their new life to be different from what they had expected. To prove this point, I will discuss the three major causes for people's disappointment with retirement. With more and more people living longer nowadays, this issue will surely become more common for many of our citizens.

d) All workers eventually retire. In some countries the retirement age is 62, while in others it is 65. Whether people are in their early 60s or late 60s when they stop working, they should have definite ideas about what this new period in their lives should be like. Some hope to spend their time with their families. Others start to make plans to travel to places around the world they had previously seen only in pictures. There are even people who decide that this is the time to resume their studies and look into various college and adult education programs. No matter what people decide is appropriate for their "golden years," they should make every effort to make the most of them.

1. Which introductory paragraph is the least interesting? Why is it uninteresting?
2. Which introductory paragraph does not state the topic of the essay?
3. Which introductory paragraph uses a story to introduce the topic?
4. Which introductory paragraph states the main points the writer intends to include in the essay?
5. Which introductory paragraph(s) do you think are effective?

2 **Choose one of these topics and develop it into an essay.**

1. The positive and/or negative effects on family life when both parents work
2. The "golden years" of retirement
3. How to "sell yourself" to a prospective employer
4. In the working world, it is not what you know but who you know that counts.

Language Summary

Part 1: Relative clauses with expressions of quantity

Example: It seems easier and more profitable for employers to hire fewer employees for longer hours rather than more employees, *each of whom would also receive health insurance and other benefits.*

Meaning: Relative clauses with expressions of quantity are non-defining. (See Unit 1.)

Form: This type of relative clause contains an expression of quantity with *of* (*all of, some of, any of, none of, both of, several of, enough of, many of, few of, the majority of,* etc.) and *whom, which,* or *whose.* It is more common in formal English, and there is a comma at the beginning and end of the relative clause.

> We've interviewed hundreds of couples, *many of whom have little time to spend with each other.*
> There have been many studies, *the majority of which prove this point.*
> These couples, *few of whose parents ever worked so much,* often talk about what they think of as the "good old days."

Part 2: Reduced adverb clauses of time

Form: When the subject of an adverb clause of time is the same as the subject of the main clause, the subject and the form of the verb *be* can be omitted.

> Most people are now working more than ever before, *while still struggling to meet their economic commitments.* (=while they are still struggling to meet their economic commitments)

Points to remember:

a) If there is no form of the verb *be* in the adverb clause, the verb can be changed to *-ing.*

> Too many of us are trying to squeeze more into each day *while having less to show for it.* (=while we have less to show for it)

b) Only adverb clauses of time that begin with these time words — *while, after, before,* and *since* — can be changed in this way.

> *Since becoming so addicted to shopping,* people have less time to devote to just "doing nothing." (=since people have become so addicted to shopping)

Part 3: Making logical deductions

Present time

1. Form: *must (not)* + *be* + present participle
> He *must be taking* the children to school. (=I'm almost sure, but not completely sure, that he's taking the children to school.)

Meaning: This form is used to express a strong degree of certainty about an action in progress at the time of speaking.

2. Form: *must (not)* + base form of the verb
> The woman can't find her report. She *must be* worried.

Meaning: This form is used to express a strong degree of certainty about an action or situation that is true at the time of speaking.

Past time

1. Form: *must (not)* + *have* + past participle
> I *must have put* the report in my briefcase. (=I'm almost sure, but not completely sure, that I put the report in my briefcase.)

2. Form: *must (not)* + *have been* + present participle
> The director *must have been talking* to his wife when I came into the office. Who else would he call "Honey"? (=I'm almost sure, but not completely sure, that he was talking to his wife.)

Meaning: These forms are used to express a strong degree of certainty about an action or situation that happened in the past.

Points to remember:

a) *Must* expresses a stronger degree of certainty than *may* and *might.* (See Unit 2, Book A.)

> It's 7 o'clock. Don't call them now. They *may be eating* dinner.
> Don't call them now. They *must be eating* dinner. They always eat dinner at this time.

> Why don't you look in your pocket? You *might have left* the key there.
> I *must have left* the key in the car. It isn't anywhere else.

b) *Must* used in present time can express degree of certainty or necessity.

> She *must be* at the meeting. That's where she said she was going. (=I'm almost sure she's at the meeting.)

> You *must be* at the meeting on time. If you're late, we'll all have to wait. (=It's necessary that you be at the meeting on time.)

However, *must* in past time expresses only degree of certainty. *Had to* + verb expresses necessity in the past. *Didn't have to* + verb expresses absence of necessity in the past.

> They *must have worked* late. That's why the lights in the building were on until 1:00 A.M. (=I'm almost sure that they worked late.)

> They *had to work* late because the director wanted the report on her desk by the morning. (=It was necessary for them to work late.)

> They *didn't have to work* all night because they finished the report before midnight. (=It wasn't necessary for them to work all night.)

THE WORLD WE LIVE IN

Talking Point

How much do you know about the world you live in? Work with two other students. Choose the correct answer to each question.* Then compare answers with another group.

1. How many more people were alive in 1982 than in 1981?
   a) million
   b) 20.5 million
   c) 77.5 million
2. How much hazardous waste has been dumped in the 100,000 industrial landfills and disposal sites in the United States since 1960?
   a) approximately 100,000 tons
   b) approximately 10,000,000 tons
   c) approximately 500,000,000 tons
3. How many of the 35,000 pesticides introduced since 1945 have been tested for their effects on people?
   a) 10%
   b) 38%
   c) 85%
4. What is the average amount of trash that each person in the United States produces per day?
   a) less than 1 pound (=$\frac{1}{2}$ kilo)
   b) between 3 to 4 pounds (=$1\frac{1}{2}$ to 2 kilos)
   c) more than 17 pounds (=8 kilos)
5. What percentage of known varieties of apple have become extinct since 1900?
   a) over 15%
   b) over 34%
   c) over 86%
6. How many rain forest trees are cut down every hour of the day?
   a) 10,000
   b) 120,000
   c) 500,000
7. How much water does a faucet dripping at the rate of one drop per second waste a year?
   a) 26 gallons (=38 liters)
   b) 880 gallons (=3,331 liters)
   c) 2,000 gallons (=7,571 liters)

8. How much carbon dioxide is produced in a year by driving an average car 1,000 miles (=1,600 kilometers) a month?
   a) approximately 1 ton
   b) approximately 10 tons
   c) approximately 120 tons
9. How much plastic ends up in the ocean every year?
   a) nearly 100,000 tons
   b) nearly 1,000,000 tons
   c) nearly 100,000,000 tons

* All answers are based on 1991 statistics.

Reading

Before reading

1 You are going to read an article from the editorial section of *The Economist*, a British magazine. The subject of the editorial is waste disposal and what governments should do as their countries run out of landfill space in the future. Check (✓) the option you think is best to deal with the problem. If you do not like any of the options, add your own.

1. Build more incinerators[1] and waste dumps in the communities that create the greatest amount of waste.
2. Charge people according to the amount of trash they throw away.
3. Burn waste at sea.
4. Pay people who agree to allow incinerators and waste dumps to be built in their neighborhood.
5. Require recycling[2] and composting[3].
6. Subsidize[4] companies to develop simpler packaging.
7. Other (Please specify): _____

[1] incinerator: a machine for burning unwanted things
[2] recycling: the processing of waste products for reuse
[3] composting: the making of a mixture from old plant or animal matter; the mixture can later be used to put in the soil to make it richer
[4] subsidize: (of governments) to pay part of the costs of something

43

2 Read the article. Which option(s) in Exercise 1 does the editorial support?

Throwing Things Away

WHAT people buy today, they throw away tomorrow. But finding somewhere to put the rubbish[1] is becoming harder and more expensive.
5   America's Environmental Protection Agency estimates that 80% of the country's landfills will shut by 2010. Japan looks like running out of landfill space by 2005. Holland has
10 more or less run out already. Other options are no easier. The Swiss repeatedly vote against new incinerators. West Germany, which in 1988 exported 2.1m tons of rubbish to
15 East Germany, has now lost that useful dumping ground. Most industrial countries agreed two years ago to discourage shipments of hazardous waste to the Third World.
20 Britain, which has long burnt the stuff on ships in the North Sea, has promised to stop it by the end of this year. No wonder that rich-country governments increasingly think of
25 waste disposal as their most pressing environmental problem.

The problem is largely manmade. Rarely is there an absolute shortage of space to put more rubbish dumps.
30 But nobody wants a dump, or an incinerator, next door. So the piles of waste grow, while the places to pile them diminish. This affects companies in two ways. First, getting
35 rid of hazardous waste is becoming more expensive. This is partly because landfill costs have soared; and also because companies now face a lengthy paper-chase, filling in forms
40 that record every stage of their

waste's progress, from factory gate to dump. As a result, more and more companies dispose of their own hazardous waste; or they
45 (expensively) change the way they work so as to reduce the amount they create. Secondly, the difficulty of getting rid of ordinary household rubbish is driving some governments
50 to impose new obligations on companies, making them take back their products when the customer wants to be rid of them. That in turn is changing the way companies
55 design products as diverse as cardboard boxes, cars and computers.

Governments are caught between voters, who do not want more dumps
60 and incinerators, and consumers, who want to go on buying things that will one day be rubbish. Confronted by the incompatible wishes of each citizen, governments
65 often expect companies to provide the answers. Sometimes this is sensible, but not always. One grand piece of foolishness: most of America's federal environmental
70 spending goes on the pursuit of companies that once dumped hazardous waste (usually legally), to make them pay for cleaning up old sites. So far, it is mainly lawyers
75 who have cleaned up. When the law has not been broken, the cost of clearing old dumps ought to be carried by the taxpayer. As for new waste, the cost of getting rid of it
80 should rest on the companies that create it. [. . .]

Rather than subsidising* one solution, or bullying companies into adopting it, governments need to
85 tackle the root causes of the municipal-rubbish mountain. Most goods in short supply become increasingly expensive, warning people to change their ways. Not so
90 with rubbish disposal. People pay nothing to throw away an extra piece of trash. Instead, the old newspapers and bottles in the rubbish bin magically vanish when the dustmen[2]

95 cart them away. In most countries the cost is rolled into city taxes or a flat fee for the service. The first goal for policy should be to make polluters carry the true financial and
100 environmental costs of waste disposal, and then leave them to decide the most efficient response.

Several sensible American cities are experimenting with charging
105 people according to the amount they throw away. That has obvious snags: the irresponsible may toss their rubbish over the nearest hedge, and the cunning may compress their
110 rubbish at home, rather than leaving the job to the dustmen. But, as Seattle and Tacoma have shown, the main results are smaller binloads and a greater willingness to take part in
115 other waste-reducing schemes, such as recycling and composting. [. . .]

In most countries the supply of rubbish is growing but the supply of rubbish dumps is shrinking. So it is
120 not enough to reduce the supply of waste: governments also need to increase the supply of sites. One way may be to encourage local people to see these sites as a source of income.
125 Provided tough safety rules are set and policed, cities and states could look for ways to reward directly those who agreed to live near an incinerator or a waste tip[3]. Getting rid of other
130 people's rubbish has always been a perfectly respectable way to earn a living. Only when modern societies start putting a value on it will they realise* just how much it is worth.

[1] rubbish (British English): trash (American English)
[2] dustmen (British English): garbage collectors (American English)
[3] tip (British English): dump (American English)

* subsidise/realise (British English spelling)
   subsidize /realize (American English spelling)

44

Guessing meaning

3 Find the words or phrases in the reading that are similar in meaning to the definitions below. (Note: Write one word in each blank.)

1. needing immediate attention (lines 23-33) _____
2. increased greatly (lines 33-44) _____
3. force someone to accept (lines 45-57) _____
4. unable to be in agreement (lines 58-66) _____
5. made a lot of money (lines 74-86) _____ _____
6. forcing (lines 74-86) _____
7. take action about (lines 74-86) _____
8. disappear (lines 89-99) _____
9. unexpected difficulties (lines 99-106) _____
10. throw (lines 107-117) _____
11. becoming smaller (lines 117-126) _____
12. acceptable to society (lines 123-134) _____

Reference words

4 What do these words refer to?

1. *that useful dumping ground* (lines 15-16)
2. *the stuff* (line 20)
3. *This* (line 33)
4. *them* (line 51)
5. *them* (line 53)
6. *this* (line 66)
7. *it* (line 79)
8. *it* (line 133)

Comprehension check

5 Listed below is the main idea of each paragraph from the reading. Match each main idea to the correct paragraph. (Note: Be careful. There are eight choices but only six paragraphs.)

a) Reasons for the large amount of rubbish
b) Reasons waste disposal has become a serious problem
c) How governments can encourage the building of dumps and incinerators
d) Reasons consumers should change their shopping habits
e) How certain city governments are reducing the amount of waste
f) How governments have tried to deal with the problem of waste disposal
g) Reasons getting rid of hazardous waste is expensive
h) The effects of the waste disposal problem on companies

Making inferences

6 Sometimes there is information that a writer does not state but that you can logically guess from what you read. Discuss the answers to these questions.

1. Why are the wishes of citizens incompatible (lines 63/64)?
2. Why has it been foolish for the American government to make companies pay to clean up sites where they dumped hazardous waste years ago (lines 67-75)?
3. Why will the supply of rubbish continue to grow (lines 117-119)?
4. Why will certain communities agree to have incinerators or dumping grounds near their homes if they are paid?

What do you think?

7 Discuss the answers to these questions.

1. The editorial refers to waste disposal as being the problem of rich-country governments (lines 23-25). Do you agree that it is only a problem for rich countries? Why or why not?
2. Why do you think consumers do not stop buying so many things when much of what they buy eventually ends up as waste?
3. Is it true in your country that "getting rid of other people's rubbish has always been a perfectly respectable way to earn a living" (lines 129-132)?
4. Do you agree with the options for dealing with waste disposal that the editorial supports? Why or why not?
5. Should governments, companies, and individual citizens be equally responsible for dealing with the waste problem? Why or why not?

Vocabulary check

8 Answer these questions.

1. What *pressing* problems is the government of your country currently facing?
2. What should the government do to *tackle* these problems?
3. Should a husband and wife who are *incompatible* stay married?
4. Is the population of your country *shrinking*?
5. What does a *respectable* person in your society not do in public?

Language Focus 1

1 The modal verb *should* (and *ought to*) has different meanings. In Unit 2, you practiced using *should* and *ought to* to talk about expectation. *Should* and *ought to* are also used to give advice. Read each sentence. Does *should* or *ought to* in each sentence express expectation or advisability?

1. People ought to pay for what they throw away. This would help reduce the amount of waste.
2. Japan should run out of landfill space by 2005. It could be a serious problem.
3. Should people throw away things that they can still use?
4. You shouldn't be wasting so much water on washing your car. Don't you know there's a water shortage?
5. The government's new policy ought to help to solve the problem. If it doesn't work, the government will have to come up with some more ideas.

Now study the information in the Grammar Box. For further information, read Part 1 of the Language Summary on page 55.

Grammar Box 1

1. **Form:** *should (not)* + base form of the verb
   ought to
   The cost of getting rid of new waste *should rest* on the companies that create it.
   The cost of clearing old dumps *ought to be carried* by the taxpayer.

2. **Form:** *should (not)* + *be* + present participle
   ought to
   Governments *should not be subsidizing* one particular solution.

Meaning: This form is used to express advisability, to say what is right or good for people to do.

---

2 What can people do to protect the environment? Make statements with *should (not)* or *ought to* and the words below.

Examples:
reuse plastic shopping bags
People should reuse plastic shopping bags.

buy products that come in a lot of packaging
People shouldn't buy products that come in a lot of packaging.

1. use biodegradable[1] detergents
2. throw empty bottles in the trash
3. use a bicycle or public transportation whenever possible
4. buy furniture made of hardwood
5. drive fuel-efficient cars
6. cut down trees in gardens
7. spray plants with chemicals to kill insects
8. take long showers

[1] biodegradable: referring to a substance that can be broken down by the natural process of decomposition

3 Work with another student. Decide what the people in the pictures are doing that is dangerous. Use *should (not)* or *ought to*.

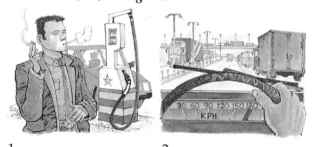

1   2

3   4

5   6

If you were near the people in the pictures, what advice would you give them?

4 Look at the information in the Grammar Box.

Grammar Box 2

Should and *ought to* also express obligation. However, the obligation is usually a moral one.

People *ought to recycle* as many things as they can.

Have to and *must*, on the other hand, express an obligation that is imposed.

In some countries people *have to separate* their trash for recycling. If they don't, they *must pay* a fine.

---

5 Talk about people in your country. Use *have to, don't have to*, or *shouldn't*. (Note: In certain situations *It's all right for people to* may also be appropriate.)

1. carry identification at all times
2. have a religious wedding ceremony
3. ask others how much money they make
4. go to someone's house uninvited
5. do military service
6. have a driver's license to be a legal driver
7. ask others who they voted for
8. stand up when the teacher walks in the room
9. be rude to a police officer
10. touch people when talking to them

Vocabulary Development 1

American English vs. British English

In the reading on page 44, there were several words used in British English. For example, people who speak British English refer to what they throw away as *rubbish*. Speakers of American English call this *trash*. The *italicized* words appear in this unit or in previous units. Try to guess their equivalents in British English from the list below and complete the sentences.

car park	clever	holiday	lorries
nappies	queue	rubbish bins	sweets
	tins	underground	

1. Americans throw things away in *trash cans*. The British use _____ .
2. American children like to eat *candy*. British children like _____ .
3. In New York people take the *subway* to work. In London people take the _____ .
4. In America there are vegetables in *cans*. In Britain these vegetables are in _____ .
5. Americans go on *vacation*. The British go on _____ .
6. Americans change their babies' *diapers* every couple of hours. The British change their babies' _____ .
7. Americans transport goods in *trucks*. The British use _____ .
8. Americans wait in a *line*. The British wait in a _____ .
9. In the United States, many cars are parked in a *parking lot*. In Britain, cars are parked in a _____ .
10. In American schools, *smart* students usually do well. In British schools, _____ students do well.

How many other British English words do you know? Make a list. Then compare lists with another student.

Language Focus 2

1 Read these two sentences. Then answer the questions.

A. People never realized what a serious problem dumping hazardous waste would become.
B. Never did people realize what a serious problem dumping hazardous waste would become.

1. Do sentences **A** and **B** have the same meaning or a different meaning?
2. Is sentence **B** a question?
3. How is sentence **B** different from sentence **A**?

Now study the information in the Grammar Box. For further information, read Part 2 of the Language Summary on page 55.

Grammar Box 3

Study the word order of the *italicized* words in these sentences.

Rarely is there an absolute shortage of space to put more rubbish dumps.
Only when modern societies start putting a value on it *will they realize* just how much it is worth.

When a negative adverb (or an adverb negative in meaning) – for example, *never, not only, rarely* – begins a sentence, the subject and verb are inverted.

---

2 Rewrite each sentence, beginning it with the *italicized* word(s).

Example: There is *rarely* an absolute shortage of space to put more rubbish dumps.
Rarely is there an absolute shortage of space to put more rubbish dumps.

1. Recycling has *never before* been so popular in so many communities.
2. Some areas started recycling *only when all the surrounding communities were recycling newspapers, bottles, and aluminum cans.*
3. Recycling is *not always* the best way to reduce the piles of municipal trash.
4. Recycling programs work *only if they are subsidized by the government.*
5. The materials that are easiest to recycle occupy the most space in landfills *only in a few cases.*
6. Recycling can be economically self-supporting *only if there is a constant demand for the recycled product.*
7. It will *never* be possible to insure that there is always a market for recycled goods.

3 Complete each sentence logically.

1. Only when the government is sure the environmental problem is serious . . .
2. Never again . . .
3. Only if there is peace throughout the world . . .
4. Under no circumstances . . .
5. At no time . . .

Listening

Before listening

1 Check (✓) the items you think are biodegradable, i.e., capable of breaking up by natural biological processes over time. Then compare answers with another student.

1. beef
2. bread wrappers
3. pastries
4. disposable diapers
5. plastic
6. a head of lettuce
7. corn on the cob
8. fingernail polish

2 You will hear an interview with an archaeologist who studies the contents of trash cans and landfills in the United States. Rank the items below from 1 to 6 (*1* being for the item you think takes up the most space in landfills he studies, *6* being for the item that takes up the least space).

a) polystyrene[1]
b) fast-food packaging
c) disposable diapers
d) plastics
e) paper
f) building waste

[1] polystyrene: a light plastic, used especially for making containers

48

Listening point

3 Listen to the interview. Write the percentage (%) of space each item takes up, according to the archaeologist.

1. polystyrene
2. fast-food packaging
3. disposable diapers
4. plastics
5. paper
6. building waste

Comprehension check

4 Answer these questions.

What evidence does the archaeologist give to show that:
1. people are more wasteful than they claim?
2. people eat less healthy food than they claim?
3. landfills preserve biodegradable waste very well?
4. it is not difficult to date material in landfills?

What do you think?

5 Discuss the answers to these questions.

1. Which parts of the interview did you find surprising?
2. Do you think a dump or landfill in your country would have the same contents as those in the United States? If not, how would they be different?
3. Would you like to be one of Professor Reynold's research assistants? Why or why not?

Vocabulary check

6 The words below were used in the interview. If you cannot remember the context in which they were used, check the tapescript. Then match the definitions in Column A with the words in Column B.

A	B
1. fill	a) *claim*
2. to keep (someone or something) alive, safe from destruction, etc.	b) *cram*
	c) *preserve*
3. declare to be true	d) *shortage*
4. an amount that is less than usual or needed	e) *take up*
5. force a person or thing into a small space	

7 Answer these questions.

1. What *takes up* the most space in your living room?
2. How important do you think it is to *preserve* historical places in your country?
3. Would most people in your country *claim* that they are not wasteful?
4. When was the last time there was a food *shortage* in your country? How about an oil *shortage*?
5. Are any of your drawers at home *crammed* with things?

Language Focus 3

1 Underline the subjects of these sentences.

1. Whatever you do affects me.
2. How old I am is none of your business.
3. What is happening to the environment should be everyone's concern.
4. That there is a serious environmental problem is a well-known fact.

Now underline the objects of these sentences.

5. We know that we must do something about the problem.
6. I don't understand what you want me to do.
7. The report didn't indicate who was responsible for the problem.

Now study the information in the Grammar Box. For further information, read Part 3 of the Language Summary on pages 55 and 56.

Grammar Box 4

1. **Form:** *that, what,*
   who,
   how old, + subject + verb + remainder
   how long, of sentence
   whatever, etc.
   I decided to find out *what the landfills contained.*

2. **Form:** *who, what,*
   which
   whoever, + subject + verb + remainder
   whatever of sentence*
   What is thought of as biodegradable is usually well-preserved.

Use: A noun clause is used in the same way as a single-word noun. Therefore, a noun clause can be the subject of a sentence.
   How long the problem will continue is anybody's guess.
   That bugs in a landfill won't eat corn on the cob is a known fact.

A noun clause can also be the object of a sentence.
   How can you tell *how old a head of lettuce is?*
   I've discovered *that 10 to 20% of fresh food is thrown away.*
   Government officials still don't know *what happened.*

* In this type of noun clause, the word that introduces the noun clause is also the subject of the verb in the noun clause. Note that the *italicized* words are the only words that can introduce this type of noun clause.

---

2 Complete each sentence by changing each question in parentheses to a noun clause.

Example: (What is a landfill?)
Do you know *what a landfill is?*

1. (What does *polystyrene* mean?)
   Can you tell me _____

2. (Does paper take up the most space in a landfill?)
   I wonder _____

3. (How does an archaeologist end up digging landfills?)
   Please tell me _____

4. (What is the name of the archaeologist?)
   I can't remember _____

5. (When did he begin studying the contents of landfills?)
   I didn't ask him _____

6. (Does he wear special clothing in the landfills?)
   You should find out _____

7. (How serious is the problem?)
   Nobody knows _____

3 Write down eight questions you would like to know the answer to. When you finish, work with another student. Ask and answer each other's questions. Be sure not to look at each other's papers. If you don't know the answer to your partner's question, say:

   I'm sorry, but I don't know _____

If you know the answer to the question, ask:

   Why do you want to know _____?

After your partner gives his or her reason, answer the question.
   Examples: (Student B does not know the answer.)

Student A: What time is it?
Student B: I'm sorry, but I don't know what time it is.

   (Student B knows the answer.)
Student A: Where did you get your watch?
Student B: Why do you want to know where I got my watch?
Student A: Because I like it and want to get one.
Student B: My parents gave it to me for my birthday.

4 Rewrite each sentence by replacing *It* with a noun clause.

   Example: It is obvious that this is one of the most serious problems facing governments around the world.
   That it is one of the most serious problems facing governments around the world is obvious.

1. It is amazing that Americans go through more than two billion batteries a year.
2. It is a well-known fact that batteries contain many hazardous materials.
3. It surprises people how much of these hazardous materials leak into landfills when batteries are thrown away.
4. It is dangerous that many of these chemicals get into our water supply.
5. It is important that people avoid throwing away batteries.
6. It is worrisome what is happening to the environment.

5 Answer these questions. Begin your answer with a noun clause. When you finish, compare answers with other students.

Example: What is uncertain?
That the government will do anything is uncertain.
OR
When the class will take the final exams is uncertain.

1. What makes your teacher happy?
2. What surprised you in this unit?
3. What have you heard or read recently that isn't true?
4. What is a well-known fact?
5. What is important to you?

Talking Point

1 Work in groups of four or five students. Talk about the three most serious environmental problems facing your country. (If you are from different countries, talk about the three most serious environmental problems facing the world.) Discuss what is being done and/or can be done to deal with each of these problems.

2 Now prepare a questionnaire for the other students in the class and your teacher. The aim of the questionnaire is to find out how much people do in their everyday lives to help tackle the three problems you discussed in Exercise 1. After everyone has completed the questionnaire, tabulate the results and report your findings to the class.

preservation of endangered species

oil spills

land erosion

air pollution

Vocabulary Development 2

Synonyms

Some words may be similar in meaning. However, that does not mean that they have the exact same meaning or that they can be used in the exact same way.

1 Match each word in Column A with its synonym(s) in Column B.

A	B
1. *claim*	a) dig up
2. *diminish*	b) get rid of
3. *dispose of*	c) grow
4. *excavate*	d) increase
5. *soar*	e) reduce
6. *toss*	f) say
	g) shrink
	h) throw
	i) throw away

2 Look at these dictionary entries for the words from Exercise 1. Then answer the questions.

claim [T] to declare to be true, especially in the face of doubt, disagreement, opposition, etc.
say [T] to express (a thought, intention, etc.)

di·min·ish [I;T] *formal* to (cause to) become or seem smaller
shrink [I;T] to become reduced in amount or value
re·duce [T] to make smaller, cheaper, etc.

dis·pose of [T] *sometimes formal* to get rid of; finish with
get rid of [T] to cause (something or someone) to go away, to be taken away, etc.
throw away [T] *informal* to get rid of (something), especially without being interested in what happens (to it)

ex·ca·vate [T] to make or uncover by breaking up and moving earth
dig up [T] to make a hole in by taking away earth, etc.

soar [I] to rise far or fast, above the normal or usual level
grow [I;T] to (cause to) get bigger, usually by progressive stages
in·crease [I;T] *often formal* to make or become larger in amount or number

toss [T] *often informal* to throw, especially lightly, without great force
throw [T] to send through the air by a sudden movement or straightening of the arm

1. Sometimes there is a grammatical difference between synonyms. For example, as you saw in Unit 5, Book A, one verb may be transitive. The other may be intransitive. Look at the grammar information that accompanies each definition. Which synonyms are different grammatically?

2. Sometimes there is a difference because a word is used in a particular style or context. Some words are used only in formal contexts while others are used only in informal contexts. Look at the dictionary entries again. Which words can be used only in certain contexts?

3. Sometimes dictionary definitions are helpful in understanding the differences between synonyms. Underline any parts of each definition that distinguish the meaning of the word from its synonym(s). Which definitions, if any, do you think are particularly helpful in understanding the differences?

3 Complete each sentence with one of the words in parentheses. If both words are correct, use both of them.

1. (claim, say)
   a) I can't _____ the answer because I don't know it.
   b) The man did _____ he had an appointment with you, but his name was not in your appointment book.

2. (diminishing, reducing)
   a) The government's popularity is _____.
   b) We are working on _____ the amount of waste we create.

3. (diminished, shrunk)
   a) The number of rain forests in the world has _____.
   b) The reputation of the company has _____ since its dumping of hazardous waste became known.

4. (dispose of, throw away)
   a) Don't _____ that paper. I need it.
   b) The company must pay to _____ all of its hazardous waste.

5. (excavated, dug up)
   a) Archaeologists have _____ a fantastic ancient city in China.
   b) You can start to plant after you have _____ the garden.

6. (soared, increased)
   a) In the past six months, prices have _____. That is why many people are finding it very difficult to feed their families.
   b) The price of the car has _____ slightly, but we can still afford to buy it.

7. (growing, increasing)
   a) The world's population is _____ by millions every year.
   b) Your hair's really _____. Aren't you going to get it cut?

8. (toss, throw)
   a) Would you _____ me those keys?
   b) Do you think you could _____ that ball 20 meters?

Writing

A. Linking words

In Unit 3 you practiced connecting sentences with linking words that show contrast. The *italicized* part in the sentence below is an example of a linking word that shows cause and effect.

> Getting rid of hazardous waste is becoming more expensive. *As a result,* more and more companies are changing the way they work in order to reduce the amount they create.

The *italicized* part in this sentence is an example of a linking word that shows addition.

> Getting rid of hazardous waste is becoming more expensive. This is partly because landfill costs have soared. *In addition,* companies now have to fill in forms that record every stage of their waste's progress.

(For rules on punctuation, see Unit 3, page 40.)

1 Does each *italicized* word express cause and effect or addition?

1. Carbon dioxide in the atmosphere acts as a blanket that traps heat from the sun. *Consequently,* too much carbon dioxide in the atmosphere is likely to lead to serious climatic effects.
2. More trees should be planted because they absorb carbon dioxide. *Furthermore,* trees produce cooling that can reduce the need for fossil fuels.
3. It is not easy to clean up the atmosphere because the problems are huge. *Moreover,* they are so complex that they are not yet fully understood, even by scientists who have studied them for years.
4. Some of the global changes happening now will be very difficult to reverse. *Therefore,* it is crucial that environmental action be taken now.

2 Complete each sentence logically.

1. People should read more about the problem. In addition, . . .
2. People are recycling more than they used to. As a result, . . .
3. Small cars are more fuel-efficient than big cars. Therefore, . . .
4. People are becoming more aware of the environmental problem. Consequently, . . .
5. The government can force companies to get rid of the waste they create. Furthermore, . . .
6. Pollution is very harmful to nature. Moreover, . . .

B. Concluding paragraphs

A well-written essay ends with a concluding paragraph that gives the reader a sense of completeness. An effective concluding paragraph:

- reemphasizes what has been said.
- relates to the general topic, not to one specific point.
- is an integral part of the essay, not a paragraph that is just added on.

1 Read these three different concluding paragraphs for an essay entitled "Joining the Struggle to Save the Earth." Then answer the questions.

a) Perhaps the most important thing that can be done to save the planet is for all of us to look around our homes and identify all the things we can do to be less wasteful. Do we really need to throw out all that trash? Do we really need to take 20-minute showers? Do we really need to turn up the heat so much? Can't we put on a sweater instead? Clearly, a little effort on our part can go a long way.

b) Around the world, people are becoming aware of the urgent need to stop destroying the environment and to start restoring it – now, before it is too late. In the United Nations and in individual countries, in political parties, in large organizations and in small community groups, people are beginning to understand the connections between their own needs and wants and the health of the whole planet. They are marching, protesting, working, and finding others to work with them. They are learning how to save the earth. You can join them.

c) In conclusion, saving the earth is obviously something that challenges us all. Something must be done before it is too late.

1. Which concluding paragraph refers to just one aspect of the struggle to save the earth?
2. Which concluding paragraph seems to be just added on to the essay rather than an integral part?
3. Which concluding paragraph leaves the reader with the strongest impression of the topic of the essay?
4. Which concluding paragraph is the most effective?

2 Look at the last essay you wrote. Is the concluding paragraph as effective as it could be? If you are not completely satisfied, rewrite it.

3 Choose one of these topics and develop it into an essay.

1. How Can the Public Become Better Informed About the Environment?
2. Now Is the Time to Tackle Pollution
3. Our Modern Way of Life Is Destroying Our World

Language Summary

Part 1: Expressing advisability / obligation

1. Form: *should (not)* + base form of the verb
      ought to

The cost of getting rid of new waste *should rest* on the companies that create it.
The cost of clearing old dumps *ought to be carried* by the taxpayer.

2. Form: *should (not)* + *be* + present participle
      ought to

Governments *should not be subsidizing* one particular solution.

Meaning: Both forms are used to express advisability, to say what is right or good for people to do. These forms are also used to express obligation. However, the obligation is usually a moral one.

Points to remember:

a) *Should* and *ought to* are similar in meaning, but *ought to* is less common and is rarely used in negative form.

b) Although *should* and *ought to* express obligation, they do not mean the same as *have to* and *must*. *Have to* and *must* express an obligation that is imposed. Compare these sentences:

People *ought to recycle* as many things as they can. (=It is the right thing to do.)
In some countries, people *have to separate* their trash for recycling, or they will pay a fine. (=It is the law.)
In some countries, people *must separate* their trash for recycling, or they will pay a fine. (=It is the law.)

c) *Shouldn't* shows that it is wrong or bad to do something. *Don't/doesn't have to* shows that it is not necessary to do something.

People *shouldn't throw away* so many things. (=It is wrong to throw away so many things.)
People are not concerned about how much they throw away because they *don't have to pay* to dispose of their trash. (=It is not necessary for people to pay.)

Part 2: Inversion of negative adverbs

Form: A negative adverb—for example, *never, not once, under no circumstances, neither, rarely, hardly ever*—is put at the beginning of the sentence. The subject and the auxiliary verb of the sentence are inverted.

Rarely is there an absolute shortage of space to put more rubbish dumps. (=There is rarely an absolute shortage of space to put more rubbish dumps.)
Never did people realize what a serious problem dumping hazardous waste would become. (=People never realized what a serious problem dumping hazardous waste would become.)

Meaning: The negative adverb appears at the beginning of a sentence to emphasize the negative element of the sentence.

Points to remember:

a) The inversion of negative adverbs is more common in written English than in spoken English.

b) There can also be inversion when restrictive phrases beginning with *only* are put at the beginning of the sentence.

Only when modern societies start putting a value on it will they realize just how much it is worth. (=Modern societies will realize just how much it is worth only when they start putting a value on it.)

c) It is necessary to insert an auxiliary if the negative adverb or *only* is brought to the beginning of the sentence.

Rarely do people complain when they are asked to recycle. (=People rarely complain when they are asked to recycle.)
Only when we didn't know about the recycling scheme did we throw away bottles and cans. (=We threw away bottles and cans only when we didn't know about the recycling scheme.)

d) There is no inversion when the negative adverbs are part of the subject.

Neither bottles nor cans should be thrown away.

Part 3: Noun clauses

Definition: A noun clause is a subordinate clause that functions as the subject or object of a sentence. Noun clauses can be replaced by *it*.

Uses:

a) Noun clauses can begin with question words—for example, *who, where, why, how, when, what, how much, how old*, etc.

I decided to find out *what the landfill contained*. (In this sentence, *what the landfills contained* is the object of the verb *find out*.)
What I discovered surprised me. (In this sentence, *what I discovered* is the subject of the sentence.)

b) Noun clauses can begin with *whether* or *if*.

People *wonder whether the government can do much about the problem*. (In this sentence, *whether the government can do much about the problem* is the object of the verb, *wonder*.)
Whether anything can be done is not clear. (In this sentence, *Whether anything can be done* is the subject.)

c) Noun clauses can begin with *that*.

People claim *that they are not wasteful*. (In this sentence, *that they are not wasteful* is the object of *claim*.)
That bugs in a landfill won't eat corn on the cob is a known fact. (In this sentence, *That bugs in a landfill won't eat corn on the cob* is the subject.)

d) Noun clauses can begin with *-ever* words—for example, *whoever, whatever, wherever, whenever*, etc.

Whoever wants to help should come to the meeting next week.
I hope you get *whatever you want*.

Points to remember:

a) Do not use question word order in noun clauses. The subject comes before the verb.

> RIGHT: Do you know what time it is?
>
> WRONG: Do you know what time is it?

b) When the noun clause is the object of the verb, *that* can be omitted, especially when speaking.

> We think that the problem can be dealt with.
>
> We think the problem can be dealt with.

When the noun clause is the subject, *that* must be included.

> RIGHT: That something needs to be done is obvious.
>
> WRONG: Something needs to be done is obvious.

c) The use of a noun clause beginning with *that* is formal. In everyday English, speakers often use *it* as the subject and put the noun clause at the end of the sentence.

> FORMAL: That the world is facing an environmental crisis is a fact.
>
> INFORMAL: It is a fact that the world is facing an environmental crisis.

SEE THE WORLD

Talking Point

If you had the money, which trips would you like to take? Check (✓) the appropriate columns. Then compare answers with other students. Be sure to explain your reasons.

	Would love to go on	Would not mind going on	Would not want to go on
1. a hunting safari in Africa			
2. a journey down the Amazon River			
3. a mountain-climbing expedition up the Himalayas			
4. a study tour of ancient ruins in Greece, Turkey, and the Middle East			
5. a trip to outer space			
6. an expedition to the Arctic			
7. a trip from Russia to China on the Trans Siberian Railroad			
8. a journey across the Atlantic on a luxury cruise liner			

Reading

Before reading

1 You are going to read an account from a book entitled *If God Wanted Us To Travel*. In the account, the writer talks about one of his top-ten hates. Rank the situations 1 to 10 in the order that each would annoy you (*1* being for the most annoying and *10* being for the least annoying).

a) Packing and unpacking suitcases
b) Waiting in airports
c) Eating airplane food
d) Being on an airplane when there's turbulence
e) Sitting in a cramped seat in the smoking section of a plane
f) Customs inspection
g) Not understanding what the people in the country are saying
h) Eating strange food
i) Having to buy gifts for friends and relatives
j) Having to get used to a different currency

57

2 Read the text. As you read, answer these questions.

1. Was the author in a good mood when he boarded the plane? Why or why not?
2. Was the author in a good mood when the plane landed at JFK Airport in New York? Why or why not?
3. Was the author in a good mood when the customs inspector finished inspecting his suitcases? Why or why not?
4. Was the author in a good mood when he left customs? Why or why not?

If God Wanted Us to Travel . . .

On every traveler's list of top-ten hates, customs has to be there. Customs inspection moves up the
5 hate list in direct proportion to how long one has been traveling and according to how much irritation one has endured during the trip.

For twenty-eight sleepless
10 hours, I had been sitting in airports listening to announcements about delayed and canceled flights, most of which were directly related to me, before I
15 managed to get the last cramped seat in the smoking section of a plane that flew across the Atlantic Ocean in record-breaking[1] turbulence, none of which
20 provided any relief for my lower back spasms[2] and three-day losing battle with dysentery[3]. As you might imagine, I was not in the best mood when we semi-crashed
25 into the torrential[4]-rain-soaked runway at JFK in the middle of the night. [. . .]

Even though I had been living these past four weeks on a rain-
30 soaked island off the Swedish coast, producing a documentary on the life of filmmaker Ingmar Bergman, housed in a small fisherman's cabin void of
35 such modern conveniences as washer and drier, I still managed to satisfy my omnipresent compulsion for neatness and cleanliness. Every article of
40 clothing in my suitcase was spotlessly clean, neatly folded, and strategically placed. Had I lived in Pompeii when the volcano erupted, I would have been racing
45 to beat the lava with a neatly packed overnight bag.

As always, the customs inspector took one look at me and asked me to open my bag. He
50 proceeded to microscopically examine everything, to the extreme of squeezing my toothpaste out of the tube. Knowing that drug smuggling is
55 a major problem, and luckily earning enough to purchase a new tube, I said nothing. I was also patient and understanding when he pulled the heel off one of
60 my shoes. However, after he tore apart my bag and found nothing, I expected him to hand it back to me in the same condition as I had handed it to him, but this was
65 not the case. What was shoved toward me was a suitcase that couldn't even be closed because of the pile of what appeared to be a bag person's[5] possessions.
70 "Next," called out the inspector.
"No next," called out this angry traveler.
"What?"
"Repack it!" I pointed to my
75 suitcase.
"You got a problem, pal?"
"You're my problem, pal," I hissed. "Get your supervisor over here, before I stuff my clothes
80 down your throat!"

I told the people behind me to change lines, because I had a feeling this was going to be a long night.
85 When the supervisor and the two New York policemen arrived, I explained how I didn't mind my bag's being scrutinized, but that I wanted it returned to me in the
90 exact condition I had handed it over. I announced that I wouldn't leave the airport until that was accomplished, and if this meant being arrested, I would surrender
95 to New York's finest[6] and talk to the press from my cell. The supervisor weighed his choices and voted in my favor. The line was officially closed and I
100 supervised the repacking of my suitcase. I'd like to say that I'm the kind of person who does not take advantage of a situation, but I cannot say it, because I am.

105 "Excuse me, but I like my socks folded, not rolled, and placed in the suitcase with the darkest colors on the bottom and the lightest on the top. . . No, my
110 underwear gets folded with the fly facing up. . . . Sorry, the pants are put on the bottom so they stay pressed, so you'll have to start over. . . . Wow, you almost have all
115 the toothpaste back in the tube . . . ."

Two hours later, I left the airport with both my suitcase and my value system intact. I was exhausted but elated. My father
120 was right when he told me as a kid, "Go to the wall on a principle." This includes airport customs' walls.

[1] record-breaking: the worst or best that has ever happened
[2] spasm: sudden pain
[3] dysentery: a stomach illness
[4] torrential: caused by violently rushing water
[5] bag person: a person who is usually homeless and who keeps his or her possessions in bags and carries the bags around all the time
[6] New York's finest: the New York police

Guessing meaning

3 Match each word in Column A with its meaning in Column B. (Note: Be careful. There are three extra choices in Column B.)

A	B
1. *void of* (line 34)	a) iron
2. *fold* (line 41)	b) examine carefully
3. *shove* (line 65)	c) without
4. *scrutinize* (line 88)	d) turn one part over another part
5. *surrender* (line 94)	e) anger
6. *take advantage* (line 103)	f) whole because no part has been damaged
7. *press* (line 113)	g) a strong feeling that you are being treated unfairly
8. *intact* (line 118)	h) very happy
9. *elated* (line 119)	i) push in a rough, careless way
	j) stop fighting and give yourself to the people you are fighting
	k) very quiet
	l) use a person or situation unfairly for one's own profit

Recognizing tone

4 Different writers use different techniques to set the tone of a story. In this story, the writer exaggerates certain parts in order to create a humorous tone. In order to understand fully a story, it is important to distinguish fact from exaggeration. Look at these words from the reading and decide if they express fact or exaggeration.

> **Examples:** *I had been sitting in airports listening to announcements about delayed and canceled flights, most of which were directly related to me.*
> (lines 10-14) *exaggeration* (Since there are many announcements at an airport, it is unlikely that over 50% of them were about the author's flights.)
> *a plane that flew across the Atlantic Ocean*
> (lines 16-18) *fact*

1. *record-breaking turbulence* (lines 18-19)
2. *none of which provided any relief for my lower back spasms* (lines 19-21)
3. *semi-crashed* (line 24)
4. *torrential-rain-soaked* (line 25)
5. *void of such modern conveniences as washer and drier* (lines 34-36)
6. *what appeared to be a bag person's possessions* (lines 68-69)

Comprehension check

5 Below are the answers to some questions about the story. Work with another student. Decide what the questions are.

1. Because he has a compulsion for neatness and cleanliness.
2. Because he was looking for drugs.
3. No, he was patient and understanding as the inspector emptied his tube of toothpaste and damaged his shoe.
4. When the inspector shoved his suitcase toward him without repacking it.
5. So that another customs inspector could check their suitcases and they wouldn't have to wait while he argued with the inspector's supervisor.
6. Because the supervisor didn't want the author to talk to newspaper and TV reporters about how customs inspectors treat travelers.
7. So that he could annoy the customs inspector as much as possible.

What do you think?

6 Discuss the answers to these questions.

1. In what way did the author take advantage of the situation (lines 101-104)?
2. What do you think the author's father meant when he said "Go to the wall on a principle" (line 121)?
3. What can you tell about the author's character based on the story?
4. Do you think that the author was right or wrong to demand that the inspector repack his suitcase? Why? Would you have done the same in his situation?

Vocabulary check

7 Answer these questions.

1. Are the clothes in your drawers at home neatly *folded*?
2. What would your reaction be if someone *shoved* you while you were waiting in line?
3. What is often *scrutinized*?
4. Do you *press* your own clothes?
5. What would make your mother or father feel *elated*?

Language Focus 1

1 Between lines 47-60 and lines 81-96 of the story on page 58, the writer includes reports of what he said to other people and what other people said to him. Underline the parts where he does this.

Now study the information in the Grammar Box. For further information, read Part 1 of the Language Summary on page 69.

Grammar Box 1

Note the changes that occur in reported speech.

a) Reporting statements:

"I don't mind my bag's being scrutinized," I explained.

I explained *how I didn't mind my bag's being scrutinized.*

b) Reporting yes/no questions:

He wanted to know, "Do you have anything to declare?"

He wanted to know *if I had anything to declare.*

c) Reporting information questions:

"Where is your supervisor?" I asked him.

I asked him *where his supervisor was.*

d) Reporting commands and requests:

"Open your bag," he said.

He asked me *to open my bag.*

---

2 Decide whether the underlined part of each sentence is right or wrong. Then correct the mistake.

Examples:

The inspector <u>asked what I h~~a~~ve</u> in my bag. *had*
wrong

I <u>told the people behind me to change lines</u>.
right

1. The couple talked to the travel agent about <u>where should they go</u> on vacation.
2. I <u>told you that you checked</u> the tickets before we left. Now we have a real problem because you didn't.
3. You told <u>us the hotel had</u> air-conditioning.
4. The flight attendant <u>asked where we did put</u> our carry-on bags.
5. When the waiter refused to let me order another dish, <u>I said that I want to talk</u> to the manager.
6. The tour guide <u>told me that this is</u> one of the best restaurants in town.

3 Rewrite this text in dialogue form.

Example: I told him to get his supervisor.
"Get your supervisor."

I told him to get his supervisor. When the supervisor arrived, he wanted to know what the problem was. I asked him to look at what the inspector had done to my bag. The supervisor replied that it was Mr. Timmons' (that was the inspector's name) job to examine all baggage thoroughly. I explained that I wanted my bag returned to me in the exact condition that I had handed it over. I announced that I wouldn't leave the airport until that was accomplished, and if this meant being arrested, I would surrender to the police and talk to the press from my cell. The supervisor responded that that wouldn't be necessary. He then told the two people who were still waiting behind me to go to another line, and ordered Mr. Timmons to repack my bag. The inspector agreed. As he started to put the things in my suitcase, I informed him that he was doing it the wrong way and would have to start all over. The inspector politely asked me how I wanted it packed, and I explained that my pants went on the bottom and the socks needed to be put inside the black shoes. When Mr. Timmons finished, he remarked that he hoped I found the repacking to my liking. I replied that I did, thanked him, and left.

4 Work with another student. Student A, listen to the tape and take notes on what the man says. Then compare notes with another Student A. Student B, listen to the tape and take notes on what the woman says. Then compare notes with another Student B. Finally, Student A and Student B, tell each other what you heard on the tape.

5 Write down five things people said to you earlier today or yesterday. Write down their names and their actual words between quotation marks. Then report what these people said to another student, who will then write down the actual words.

Example:

NAME	SENTENCE
The teacher	*"Please do exercise 5."*

Student A says *The teacher told me to do Exercise 5.* Student B should then write down, without looking at Student A's paper, Student A's words in direct speech.

Vocabulary Development 1

Reporting verbs

1 The reporting verbs in the box give more information about how the speaker spoke than *say* or *ask* do. Check with your teacher or look in a dictionary to find the meaning of any new words. Then replace *said* in each sentence with one of these words. (Note: Use each verb only once.)

> begged confessed muttered offered ordered
> protested swore threatened whispered

1. "Okay, okay, yes, I did it. I smuggled the drugs," the young woman said.
2. "He'll be sorry. Who does he think he is tearing up my suitcase like that?" the traveler said.
3. "Let me go. You can't arrest me. I know my rights," Sylvia said.
4. "Oh, Linda, I will always love you," Joe said.
5. "Put your arms up and move over to the wall. Come on. Move," the police officer said.
6. "I can tell you one thing: I'll talk to the press unless you do something," the traveler said.
7. "The drugs are not mine. You have to believe me. I'm telling you the truth," the arrested man said.
8. "Please don't report me to my supervisor," the inspector said. "I might lose my job if you do. I have a family to support. Please, I need this job."
9. "Ma'am, why don't you let me help you with that bag?" the young man said. "It looks pretty heavy."

2 Look at the different reports of what the speaker said. Then answer the questions.

1. "Lady, move. If you don't, I'll shoot."
   A. He told the woman to move. He told her that if she didn't move, he'd shoot.
   B. He threatened to shoot the woman if she didn't do what he told her to do.

2. "Please don't shoot. I'll do whatever you want me to do."
   A. The woman asked him not to shoot. She said she would do whatever he wanted her to do.
   B. The woman begged him not to shoot.

1. Which sentences report the exact words?
2. Which sentences report the central point of what the speaker has said?
3. Which do you think is better style – to report the exact words or to report the speaker's main point?

3 Report what was said in Exercise 1. Notice how the verbs are used.

> *beg* + someone + infinitive
> *order*

> *threaten* + infinitive
> *offer*

> *confess*
> *mutter*
> *protest* + *that* + noun clause
> *swear*
> *threaten*
> *whisper*

Example: "Please don't make me do it. Please," the woman said to the man.
The woman begged the man not to make her do it.

Listening

Before listening

1 Answer these questions.

1. Have you ever been to Paris? If so, what do you remember about your visit? If you haven't been to Paris, would you like to go there? What would you like to do there?
2. What five words and/or phrases do you associate with Paris?
3. If you had a friend who was preparing to go to Paris to study French, what advice would you give him or her?

Guessing meaning

2 On the tape, you will hear sentences which contain the *italicized* words. As you listen, try to guess their meaning. Then choose the meaning of each word.

1. *take pity on*
   a) help people because you feel sorry for them
   b) look at people because you find them interesting
2. *sympathetically*
   a) in a friendly way
   b) showing understanding of another person's problems
3. *Dawn was breaking.*
   a) The sun was rising.
   b) The sun was setting.
4. *drag*
   a) pull a heavy thing along
   b) carry a light thing over your shoulders
5. *give one's word*
   a) express an opinion
   b) make a promise
6. *dash*
   a) walk out slowly and calmly
   b) run quickly and suddenly
7. *relieved*
   a) feeling worry about possible problems
   b) feeling comfort at the ending of anxiety or worry
8. *instinct*
   a) a natural understanding
   b) information from doing research

Listening point

3 Listen to the story.* Then choose the best title for the story.

a) Lost in Paris
b) Springtime in Paris
c) Timeless in Paris
d) Romance in Paris

*You will hear the following words in French in the story:

Gare du Nord: the name of a train station in Paris
Pas de chambres: no rooms
Monsieur l'Anglais: Mr. Englishman
the tenth *arrondissement:* an area of Paris

Comprehension check

4 Find the mistakes in this summary of the story. Cross out the parts that are wrong and correct them.

The speaker went to Paris hoping to improve his French by meeting young French women. He arrived in the early hours of the evening and because he had reserved a hotel room from England, he went straight to the hotel. When he got there, he learned that his room had been given by mistake to someone else, so he had to spend much of the time before daybreak looking for a room. He finally found a hotel, but since there were no rooms until later in the day, he went to bed in the breakfast room. He slept for a few hours and then went out for a walk until his room was ready for him. He finally went to sleep in the evening thinking that he would wake up the next morning in time to get to his appointment. When he woke up, it was 7:30. As he had to be at the meeting place at 8:00, he rushed to get there on time. When he got there a few minutes early, he was surprised to see that the building where he was to go was still closed and that there were no other young men also waiting. He waited and waited. By 8:30, the thought suddenly came to him that maybe it wasn't 8:30 in the morning but 8:30 in the evening. He was confused and tried to figure out where he was.

What do you think?

5 Discuss the answers to these questions.

1. What would your reaction be if someone came up to you on the street and said to you, "Excuse me. Could you tell me if it's Monday or Tuesday?"
2. If you had been in a situation similar to that of the speaker, would you:
   a) have spent the night in the train station or gone out to look for a hotel room at 1 A.M.? Why?
   b) have agreed to spend the night in the break-fast room or accepted the offer of the hotel worker's room? Why?
   c) have made a hotel reservation before going to Paris or waited until you arrived in the city? Why?
3. Which parts of the story are typical of a traveler's experience? Which are unusual?

Vocabulary check

6 Answer these questions.

1. Would you *take pity on* a person who was hungry and offer him or her a meal?
2. Did your teacher listen *sympathetically* the last time you had a problem?
3. Would you be able to carry a suitcase that weighed 25 kilos or would you have to *drag* it?
4. How do you feel when someone who has *given his or her word* doesn't keep it?
5. If you were lost, would you rely on your *instinct* to find the right way or would you ask someone for directions?

Talking Point

Prepare notes to talk to the class for four or five minutes on one of these subjects:

1. A memorable event on a trip or excursion you took
2. A famous place in your country
3. An aspect of your culture that would interest foreign visitors

When you have finished your talk, other students should ask you questions.

Language Focus 2

1 Read these two sentences. Then answer the questions.

> **A.** I *should have paid* more attention to finding a place to stay before I left for Paris.
> **B.** I *should have left* my bags at the station while I went to look for a room.

1. What time is referred to in each sentence – past, present, or future?
2. Did the actions happen – that is, did the speaker in sentence **A** pay more attention; did the speaker in sentence **B** leave his bags?
3. What meaning does *should have* + past participle express?

Now study the information in the Grammar Box. For further information, read Part 2 of the Language Summary on page 70.

Grammar Box 2

1. **Form:** *should (not)* + *have* + past participle
   I *should have paid* more attention to finding a place to stay before I left for Paris. (=I was wrong not to pay more attention to finding a place to stay before I left for Paris.)

   Meaning: This form is used to say that someone did the wrong thing.

2. **Form:** *should (not)* + *have been* + present participle
   I *shouldn't have been walking* the streets of Paris at 3:00 A.M. I was lucky nothing happened to me. (=I was wrong to be walking the streets of Paris at 3:00 A.M.)

   Meaning: This form is used to say that someone was doing the wrong thing.

2 Jerry had a terrible day yesterday. Use *should* to say what he did wrong.

Example: He got up late because he turned the alarm off and went back to sleep.
He shouldn't have gone back to sleep.

1. He got soaking wet in the rain because he didn't bring an umbrella.
2. The person he was supposed to meet at 9:00 left before he got to the office because he forgot to call to say he would be late.
3. When Jerry's manager came into his office, Jerry wasn't working. He was talking on the phone about last night's football game.
4. He fell down the stairs because he wasn't looking where he was going.
5. He drove through a red light because he wasn't paying attention. He got a ticket for $100.
6. His girlfriend is furious with him because when she arrived at the movie theater, he was talking to another woman.
7. He had four cups of coffee before he went to bed. Then he couldn't sleep.

3 What did these people probably say about their mistakes? Answer the questions using *should*. When you finish, compare answers in groups.

Example: What did the student say when she got a bad grade on an exam?
I should have studied harder.

1. What did the prisoner say to himself as he looked out the window of his prison cell?
2. What did an employee who was just fired say to one of her co-workers?
3. What did the famous tennis player say in front of the TV camera after she had lost an important match?
4. What did the driver of one car that had just been in an accident say to the driver of the other car?
5. What did the divorced man say to a friend shortly after he received his divorce papers?

4 Make true statements with *should* about mistakes you or other people have made in any of the areas in the box. When you finish, tell another student what you wrote and explain the context.

Examples: Home

I should have taken all the tissues out of the pockets of my clothes before I washed them. My clothes were a mess when I took them out of the washing machine.

My husband shouldn't have been talking on the phone while he was cooking. He didn't notice that the telephone cord was next to the hot oven. The cord melted, and then the phone stopped working.

Family
Friends
Health
Home
Politics
Travel
Work

Vocabulary Development 2

Parts of the body as verbs

Verbs can be formed from several words for parts of the body.

Example:
I expected him to *hand* it back to me in the same condition as I had *handed* it to him.

1 **Look up in your dictionary these words for parts of the body. Write X if the word is not used as a verb. If the word is used as a verb, write down the number of meanings it has in its verb form.**

1. arm	5. foot	9. nose
2. back	6. hair	10. shoulder
3. ear	7. hand	11. stomach
4. face	8. head	12. teeth

2 **Complete each sentence with one of the words in the box. (Note: There are nine choices but only seven sentences.)**

arm	back	face	foot	hand	head
	nose	shoulder	stomach		

1. *A:* I don't know how you can _____ this food. It's awful.
   B: It's not so bad. The food we had yesterday was worse.

2. *A:* Isn't the restaurant you want to go to expensive?
   B: Yes, but I intend to _____ the bill. You're my guest.

3. *A:* What do you think, should we turn here or go straight?
   B: _____ it. We're hopelessly lost. We'll have to go back to town and get directions.

4. *A:* Excuse me. Can you tell me if the Grand Hotel is near here?
   B: You've gone one street too far. _____ up to the corner and turn left.

5. *A:* What does he want? Do you understand him?
   B: I think he wants you to _____ him your passport so that he can write down your name.

6. *A:* Did you see a group of tourists pass by?
   B: Yes. If you want to find them, you should _____ that way. They turned down that street about ten minutes ago.

7. *A:* Don't _____ around in there. We may get into trouble.
   B: Why? I only want to see what's in the box. I'm not going to take anything.

Language Focus 3

1 **Read the postcard that David, the speaker you heard on tape, sent to a friend in England. He mentions two things he's sorry he did or didn't do. Underline them.**

Dear Annie,   29 April

Greetings from Paris! Arrived a couple of days ago and enrolled in the language school yesterday. You were right. I wish I had listened to you. I had a terrible time finding a place to stay. Believe it or not, the first night I spent in a bed in the breakfast room of a hotel!
You were right about one other thing too — the suitcases. I wish I hadn't brought so much stuff. Believe me, it was no fun dragging them all around at three in the morning.
Oh well, all's well that ends well. Hope you enjoy saying "I told you so" to yourself.
love
David

Annie Kay
98 Queens Drive
Berrylands, Surbiton
Surrey KT5 8PP
ANGLETERRE

Now study the information in the Grammar Box. For further information, read Part 3 of the Language Summary on page 70.

Grammar Box 3

Form: *wish* + past perfect (or past perfect progressive)

I wish I had listened to you.
(=I'm sorry that I didn't listen to you.)

Meaning: This form is used to express regrets about events or situations that happened (or did not happen) in the past. (Note that this meaning is different from the meaning of *wish* you practiced in Unit 1, Book A. See page 8.)

---

2 Here are some other excerpts from postcards. Complete them with the correct form of the verbs in parentheses.

1. Having a great time. Both of us wish you _____ (be) here.

2. I wish you _____ (can see) this place. You'd love it.

3. It's very hot here at this time of year. I wish I _____ (come) in the spring when it's cooler.

4. It's been such a relaxing vacation. I wish we _____ (not have to leave) so soon. Unfortunately, we've got only a few days left.

5. Last night we went to a disco, and Bill danced for hours. I wish you _____ (see) him. It was so funny.

6. The sun is bright, and the sea is blue. We wish you _____ (be able to come) with us. It's too bad you couldn't. Maybe next year.

7. Yesterday was shopping day. I had a great time, but I wish I _____ (not buy) so much because now I don't have much money left.

3 The people in the pictures are all sorry about things they did or didn't do. What are they probably saying to themselves at the moment? Make sentences with *wish*.

Examples:
I wish I had reserved a room in advance.
OR
I wish I had called first.

1   2

3   4

Writing

A. Participial phrases

In Unit 5, Book A, you saw that participial phrases beginning with a past participle are used in formal writing. The following sentence from the reading on page 58 contains an example of a participial phrase that begins with a present participle.

Knowing that drug smuggling is a problem, I said nothing.

Remember that the implied subject (*I*) of the participial phrase is usually the same as the subject of the sentence (*I*). The sentence means the same as: I knew that drug smuggling was a problem, so I said nothing.

1 Decide whether each sentence is right or wrong. Then correct the mistake.

Examples:
a) Not knowing the correct way to go, I stopped a stranger to ask for directions. *right*
(This sentence is correct; the implied subject of the participial phrase, *I*, is the same as the subject of the sentence.)
b) Walking down the street, a huge branch struck me on the head. *wrong*
(This sentence is wrong. It means that a *huge branch*, the subject of the sentence, was walking down the street. This is incorrect because branches of trees do not walk.)
As I was walking down the street, a huge branch struck me on the head.

1. Not having reserved a room in advance, the young tourist had to spend the night sleeping in the park.
2. Reading a book about traveling, all the places I could travel to filled my mind with wonder.
3. Sitting behind the reception desk with an angry look on his face, I wondered if I should bother asking the man if he had a room.
4. Admiring the sight, the time and effort that went into its creation filled me with wonder.

2 Rewrite these sentences using a participial phrase.

Example: My brother's not much of a traveler, so he rarely leaves our hometown.
Not being much of a traveler, my brother rarely leaves our hometown.

1. Because I can't understand why anyone would want to go camping, I laughed when my friends said that that was what they were going to do for their vacation.
2. My fiancé and I wanted to decide where to go on our honeymoon, so we went to see a travel agent.
3. We didn't have any idea what the weather would be like, and we brought all the wrong clothes.
4. As I opened the front door of my house after two months abroad, I thought to myself, "There's no place like home."

B. Developing a story

When telling a story, it is important for the writer to give as many details as possible so that the reader feels like part of the scene.

1 Read the skeleton of a story below. The story is about being lost in the desert and was originally in seven paragraphs. Then decide with one or two other students what details to add to make the story more interesting. You may want to add details based on answers to the questions.

1. He gave us a choice of riding a minibus to the temple or taking a walk through the fields.
a) Who gave you the choice?
b) What nationality was he?
c) Where were you?
d) What time of the day was the walk?

2. He gave me instructions. It was very simple: I merely had to climb up an embankment[1], the only embankment, and follow the dirt road, the only dirt road.
e) What were the instructions for?
f) Was the embankment big or small?
g) Where was the dirt road?

3. The road was there, exactly as he had described. After walking, I instinctively knew that I was not on the correct road.
h) Where was the road?
i) After how much walking?
j) How were you walking?

[1] embankment: a wide wall which is built to hold back water

4. Playing nearby were four children, three boys and a girl. The girl was already a dark beauty. I approached them.
k) What nationality were the children?
l) What ages were they?
m) What did the girl look like?

5. With words and gestures, I was able to ask. They shook their heads and pointed to a field.
n) What were you able to ask?
o) Did they shake their heads simultaneously or at different times?
p) Where was the field?

6. As we walked along together, they were having a grand time. When we came out of the field, we were standing on a road. They pointed. I reached into my pocket and handed each one something.
q) What were they doing that caused them to have a grand time?
r) What kind of road?
s) What did they point toward?
t) What did you hand them?

7. I stood in front of it. He ran up to me, told me something, and he apologized.
u) When did you stand in front of it?
v) What did you stand in front of?
w) Who ran up to you?
x) What did he tell you?

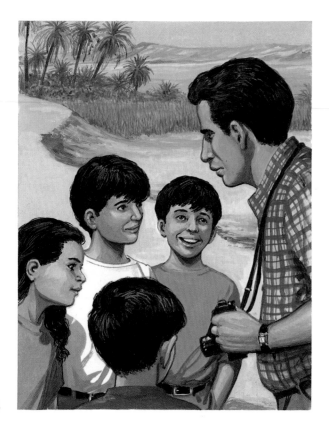

68

2 Below are the final parts of each paragraph of the story in Exercise 1. Match each part with the correct paragraph.

a) The three boys babbled[1] some kind of thanks; the little girl added a hug.

b) Ridiculous, right? The guide had been bringing tours here for the past twelve years. He had pointed to the only embankment, which I had climbed, and I was walking along the only dirt road there, so how could it possibly be wrong? It couldn't, but I knew for some inexplicable reason that it was.

c) The girl explained with her rather limited English vocabulary that the two smaller boys were her brothers and the oldest boy, if I was interpreting her facial expression and tone correctly, wasn't to be trusted.

d) It seems that this was the first time the cruise ship had not docked in its usual spot. There was no way he could tell the difference; the embankment was identical, and coincidentally had an identical dirt road at the top of it. Only when he was on the minibus did he realize it. He asked how I managed to find the right road. I smiled and shrugged.

e) I always prefer walking to riding, especially in foreign countries. You see so much more and get a better feel for the life of the people.

f) These were my kind of directions.

g) They volunteered to take me through the tall grass to what I assumed was the right road. I signaled for them to lead the way.

[1] babble: speak a meaningless confusion of words

3 Now rewrite the story. Incorporate the details you added in Exercise 1 and the final parts in Exercise 2. When you finish, compare stories with another group.

4 Write about a memorable incident you had during:
a) a trip abroad;
        OR
b) a trip to another part of your country;
        OR
c) an excursion to a nearby town.

Describe it in detail so that the reader will be able to feel that he or she is part of the story.

Language Summary

Part 1: Reported speech

Meaning: Reported speech is used to report what another person has said.

Reporting statements
Form:

a) If the reporting verb (for example, *said, told, explained,* etc.) is in the past, the tense of the verb in the reported statement usually changes.

DIRECT SPEECH	REPORTED SPEECH
simple present (*does*)	➡ simple past (*did*)
present progressive (*is doing*)	➡ past progressive (*was doing*)
present perfect (*has done*)	➡ past perfect (*had done*)
simple past (*did*)	➡ past perfect (*had done*) or simple past

"I don't mind my bag's being scrutinized," I explained.
I explained *how I didn't mind my bag's being scrutinized.*

"I don't want to argue with you," I told him.
I told him *that I didn't want to argue with him.*

b) If the reporting verb is in the past but the statement refers to a fact that is still true, the tense of the verb in the reported statement often does not change.

He said, "I hate customs inspectors."
He said *he hates customs inspectors.* (He still hates customs inspectors, so it is not necessary to change the tense.)

"Not everyone's bags are inspected in such a manner," she informed us.
She informed us *that not everyone's bags are inspected in such a manner.* (This is a general fact and is true in the present, so it is not necessary to change the tense.)

c) If the reporting verb is in the present, the tense of the verb in the reported statement does not change.

"I'll be there in a minute."
The supervisor says *he'll be here in a minute.*

Points to remember:
a) Some modal verbs change.

will	➡	*would*
can	➡	*could*
must (necessity)	➡	*had to*

"I won't repack your bag," he said.
He told me *he wouldn't repack my bag.*
Other modal verbs do not change.
My wife said, "You shouldn't argue with the official."
My wife told me *I shouldn't argue with the official.*

b) *Tell* is always used with an indirect object, i.e., the person spoken to. *Say* is rarely used with an indirect object.
RIGHT: He told me that he had made a mistake.
WRONG: He said me that he had made a mistake.

c) *That* in reported speech is optional.
He said that he would get the supervisor
OR
He said he would get the supervisor.

Reporting questions
Form: If the reporting verb (*asked, wanted to know,* etc.) is in the past, the tense of the verb in the reported question usually changes, as it does with reported statements.

"Do you have anything to declare?" the inspector asked.
The inspector wanted to know *if I had anything to declare.*

I asked, "Where is your supervisor?"
I asked him *where his supervisor was.*

Points to remember:
a) When reporting *yes/no* questions, the report begins with *if* or *whether* and the word order is no longer that of a question.
"Are you going to repack my bag?"
RIGHT: I asked if he was going to repack my bag.
WRONG: I asked if was he going to repack my bag.

b) When reporting questions beginning with question words (*where, why,* etc.), the word order is no longer the word order of a question.
"Why are you squeezing the toothpaste out of the tube?"
RIGHT: I asked why he was squeezing the toothpaste out of the tube.
WRONG: I asked why was he squeezing the toothpaste out of the tube.

c) When reporting questions, the auxiliary (*do, does, did*) is not used.
RIGHT: He asked where I come from.
WRONG: He asked where do I come from.

Reporting commands and requests
Form: When reporting commands and requests, the infinitive form is used and follows this pattern:

Subject	+	Reporting Verb	+	Indirect Object	+	Infinitive
He		told		me		to open my bag.

Points to remember:
a) Notice the position of *not* in reported commands and requests.
"Don't speak to me in that manner!"
I told the inspector *not to speak to me in that manner.*

b) Words such as *please* are not common in reported speech.
"Would you please change lines?" I asked.
I asked *the people behind me to change lines.*

Part 2: Criticizing (past time)

1. Form: *should (not) + have + past participle*

I *should have paid* more attention to finding a place to stay before I left for Paris. (=I was wrong not to pay more attention to finding a place to stay before I left for Paris.)

Meaning: This form is used to say that someone did the wrong thing. It implies that the action didn't happen.

He *shouldn't have said* there was a room since the hotel had been fully booked for a week. (But he did.)

2. Form: *should (not) + have been + present participle*

I *shouldn't have been walking* the streets of Paris at 3:00 A.M. I was lucky nothing happened to me. (=I was wrong to be walking the streets of Paris at 3:00 A.M.)

Meaning: This form is used to say that someone was doing the wrong thing. It shows that the action had duration.

Point to remember:

In addition to *should*, *ought to* can be used to criticize past actions, but *should* is more common. *Ought to* is rare in questions and negatives.

I *ought to have paid* more attention to finding a place to stay before I left for Paris.

Part 3: Expressing regrets (past time)

Form: *wish + past perfect (or past perfect progressive)*

I *wish I had listened* to you. (=I'm sorry that I didn't listen to you.)

Meaning: This form is used to express regrets about events or situations that happened (or did not happen) in the past.

Points to remember:

a) Even though you are referring to past time, you cannot use the simple past after *wish* to express regrets.

RIGHT: I wish I had reserved a room before I arrived in Paris.

WRONG: I wish I reserved a room before I arrived in Paris.

b) *That* after *wish* is optional.

I wish that I hadn't brought so much stuff.

I wish I hadn't brought so much stuff.

LIVE AND LEARN

Talking Point

Read each statement below and check (✓) the appropriate column. When you finish, compare answers with three or four other students. Be sure to give the reasons for your answers.

	Strongly agree	Agree somewhat	Don't agree or disagree	Disagree somewhat	Strongly disagree
Going to school can be harmful to children.					
Children only learn by attending school.					
People cannot succeed in life without an education.					
All children should be required by law to attend school.					
Teaching is an act of love.					
Schools are sometimes like prisons.					
Parents should help children with their schoolwork.					
It is important that teachers maintain discipline in the classroom.					
Students should not have to take required subjects. They should learn a subject when they show an interest in it.					

Reading

Before reading

1 This unit's reading was written by a high school teacher and is entitled "When Schools Fail Children." In the article, the writer describes certain aspects of what happens at the typical American high school. Check (✓) the statements which are true about high schools in your country.

1. There are approximately 30 students in a class.
2. Students change classrooms, teachers, and subject matter every hour or so.
3. Students in the same grade are usually of the same age and social class.
4. Students attend school 30 hours a week, 36 weeks a year.
5. Students do seven to ten hours of homework a week.

2 When you want to get a general idea about the contents of an article, it is helpful to read the first sentence of each paragraph. Each sentence below is the first sentence of a paragraph from this unit's reading. Read the sentences and write down what you think the article is about.

(Paragraph 2) Could there be something in the very nature of the school as an institution that prevents it from fully realizing its mandate to inform, educate, and develop both the individual and his or her society?

(Paragraph 3) My students are compelled to herd themselves from room to room, to sit in daily confinement with other people of precisely their age and approximately their social class, to hear me whether or not they are ready.

(Paragraph 4) Admittedly, as a professional educator, I am part of this vast bureaucracy.

(Paragraph 5) Yet for all this, for all the quiet joys of the classroom, it seems to me that many of my students should simply be elsewhere, that they would be better served by a different sort of education, that their society would be better served by it, too.

(Paragraph 6) It is for this reason that I am a walking contradiction.

(Paragraph 7) I wish I could write that my wife and I had excellent reasons for deciding to homeschool.

(Paragraph 8) There are hours in the morning—two, at most—when my wife sits down with our nine-year-old and is systematic about writing and mathematics.

(Paragraph 9) Their education is various, alive, participatory, whole—and, most of all, *theirs*.

3 Read the article. Was your prediction in Exercise 2 correct?

WHEN SCHOOLS FAIL CHILDREN

Never let your schooling get in the way of your education, advised the famous American author, Mark Twain, who never attended school.

Could there be something in the very nature of the school as an institution that prevents it from fully realizing its mandate to inform, educate, and develop both the individual and his or her society? At the high school where I teach, as at most, students come and go in sets of thirty or so at approximately one-hour intervals, an arrangement convenient to the daunting task of administering a crowd of more than 800 young people but not necessarily conducive to their education or in the best interests of society.

My students are compelled to herd themselves from room to room, to sit in daily confinement with other people of precisely their age and approximately their social class, to hear me whether or not they are ready. They are scrutinized, sorted, graded, disciplined, and their waking hours are consumed by this prison life: thirty hours a week, thirty-six weeks a year, seven to ten hours a week of "homework" twelve years running—the heart of their young lives consumed by it.

Admittedly, as a professional educator, I am part of this vast bureaucracy. Yet I see no contradiction in what I am doing; coming each day to where young people are, attempting within the constraints of the institution to see to their education. Each year I come to admire many of my students, to like them so well that I am sad to see them go.

Yet for all this, for all the quiet joys of the classroom, it seems to me that many of my students should simply be elsewhere, that they would be better served by a different sort of education, that their society would be better served by it, too. I believe this education is one their parents can best provide and that they should expect schools to assist them. These parents love their children with a depth that, finally, I can't match—and finally, teaching is an act of love before it is anything else.

It is for this reason that I am a walking contradiction. I teach my neighbors' children in my high school classroom, but my wife and I teach ours at home.

I wish I could write that my wife and I had excellent reasons for deciding to homeschool. We didn't. But as it turns out, it is a life our family likes, and this is our chief reason for continuing to homeschool. Our days and our children's days are various. They pass with no sense that learning is separate from life, an activity that begins at a specific point in the morning and arbitrarily ends at another in the afternoon. Instead, learning proceeds from our children, spurred by their interests and questions. A winter day on which snow falls is the natural starting point of discussion and reading about meteorology, weather fronts, Alaska, polar bears. A spring evening spent on a blanket in the yard as the stars begin to show themselves is a proper time for talk of constellations, for bringing out a star chart, for setting up a telescope, for questions about satellites, the Apollo space program. When the weather is poor for roaming out of doors, our boys—five, seven, and nine—might spend hours playing Scrabble or chess, or read to one another, or draw pictures,or comb through atlases and encyclopedias because the maps and pictures interest them.

There are hours in the morning—two, at most—when my wife sits down with our nine-year-old and is systematic about writing and mathematics; later, they will practice violin together. Evenings are my time for nurturing our children's interest in geography, for discussing the day's news, and for reading poems to them before they go to bed. We try to be consistent about these matters, and yet no two days are ever much alike. [. . .]

Their education is various, alive, participatory, whole—and, most of all, *theirs*. Quite frankly, no school can hope to match it. They have not learned to be fearful of learning, to associate it with pain and dreariness, with competition, anxiety, dread.

Guessing meaning

4 **Study how the words below are used in the reading on page 73. Then complete each sentence that follows with one of the words.**

daunting (line 16)   *arbitrarily* (line 79)
conducive (line 19)   *comb* (line 102)
contradiction (line 39)   *consistent* (line 116)
constraint (line 42)   *dread* (line 126)

1. For some children the first day at school is one full of _____ . When they say good-bye to their mother or father, you can see great fear on their faces.

2. For people with learning problems, being successful in school can be _____ . Everything seems difficult, and they get discouraged easily.

3. Schools are not always _____ to successful learning because it is difficult for students to concentrate when they are in a small space with 30 other people.

4. There are many limitations to what a teacher can do for slower students. One _____ is time: when the 50-minute period is over, the students must go to the next class.

5. Don't you see the _____ ? You say education is important, yet you refuse to pay the taxes the government needs to give children a good education.

6. I _____ed through the book, but I couldn't find the information. I'm sure it's not there because I looked very carefully.

7. Our book is _____ . It begins with a reading text. Then it practices grammar. In this regard, all the units are the same.

8. I didn't have any reason for deciding to take that course. I had to take five courses and that one I chose _____ . It turned out to be great.

Comprehension check

5 **Below are the main ideas for paragraphs 2 to 9. Match each main idea with the correct paragraph. Paragraph 2 has been done for you.**

a) Students would be better off if their parents taught them.
b) It's difficult for students to learn in the environment of a school.
c) The writer and his wife do certain subjects on a regular basis.
d) Schools cannot educate students because of the way schools are set up. *2*

e) The writer's children have a very varied education.
f) The writer's children get a better education at home than they could get at a school.
g) Although the writer realizes that schools are not perfect, he still gets satisfaction as a teacher in one of them.
h) The writer teaches other people's children at school, but his own children do not attend school. The writer teaches his children at home.

What do you think?

6 **Discuss the answers to these questions.**

1. Do you think you would have received a better education if your parents had taught you at home? Why or why not?
2. What kind of problems do you think the writer's children may face because they are being educated at home?
3. Do you think that parents who want to educate their children at home should be allowed by law to do so? Why or why not?
4. Do you agree with the writer that "the heart of [students'] young lives" are consumed by school? Why or why not?
5. The writer sees several problems with educating children in school. On a scale of 1 to 10 (*1* being not serious and *10* being very serious), how serious do you think these problems are?

a) Students are graded.
b) Students are disciplined.
c) Students must sit for many hours.
d) Students have to listen to the teacher, whether they are ready or not.
e) Students must do homework.
f) Students must learn in large groups.
g) Students must stop learning about a subject at the end of the hour, whether they are ready to stop or not.
h) Students are tested.

Vocabulary check

7 **Look back at your completed sentences in Exercise 4. Then write a definition, synonym, or translation for each word below. (If you write down a translation, check a bilingual dictionary to see if you guessed correctly.)**

1. dread   4. constraint   7. consistent
2. daunting   5. contradiction   8. arbitrarily
3. conducive   6. comb

Now circle the parts of each sentence in Exercise 4 which helped you guess the meaning of the words.

Language Focus 1

1 Complete the story by adding *a* or *an*, *the*, or Ø if no article is needed.

. . . _____ spring evening spent on _____ blanket in _____ yard as _____ stars begin to show themselves is a proper time for talk of _____ constellations, for bringing out _____ star chart, for setting up _____ telescope, for _____ questions about satellites, _____ Apollo space program. When _____ weather is poor for roaming out of doors, our boys might spend hours playing Scrabble or chess, or read to one another, or draw _____ pictures, or comb through _____ atlases and _____ encyclopedias because _____ maps and pictures interest them.

Now check your answers on page 73 between lines 88 and 104. Then work out with another student why the writer used the indefinite article, the definite article, or no article in these sentences.

Now study the information in the Grammar Box. For further information, read Part 1 of the Language Summary on page 83.

Grammar Box 1

1. The indefinite article *a* or *an* is used to refer to a singular count noun that is NOT specified or identified as a particular one.

    There's *a student* waiting to see you outside. (=We do not know which particular student this is.)

2. The definite article *the* is used to refer to a noncount noun or a singular or plural count noun that has been specified or identified.

    There's a student waiting to see you. *The student* said you told her to wait. (=We know which student this is.)

3. No article is used for a plural count noun or a noncount noun when these nouns refer to people, objects, ideas, etc., in general.

    Do *schools* fail *children*?

---

2 The person who typed the following paragraphs left out *a* and *the*. Read the paragraphs, and add *a* and *the* where necessary. (Note: In the original text, *a* appeared twice and *the* appeared eleven times.)

"Parents in this community think education is teachers' responsibility. They send child to school and they expect school to do everything." Maria Hidalgo is describing challenge facing Westmont High School in El Paso, Texas, in its efforts to involve parents.

School gets its students from one of poorest parts of city. Seventy percent are Mexican-Americans. Some mothers do not speak English. They did not go to school themselves and do not understand American system.

Next September school's 700 students will have homework diary so that parents will know what homework has been assigned and will be able to comment on how easy or difficult their children find assignments. Diary is result of conversations with parents about homework.

3 People have different values and goals in life. Check (✓) the three values and goals that are most important to you and the three that are least important to you. Compare answers with other students, and give the reasons for your answers. Be sure to use the indefinite and definite articles correctly in your discussion.

	Most Important	Least Important
Adventure		
Financial security		
Personal growth		
Approval from others		
Knowledge		
Enjoyment of beauty		
Success in a career		
Friendship		
Helping others		
Having fun		
Recognition and respect		
Cooperation		
Power		
Independence		
Equality		
Responsibility for others		
Moral goodness		
Privacy		

Vocabulary Development 1

Dictionary skills

Some nouns are countable [C] when they have one meaning and are uncountable [U] when they have another meaning. Some nouns are countable but appear only in singular form [S].

1 The words below appeared in the reading on page 73. Study the grammar information which comes before each definition.

class 1 [U] the fact that there are different social groups with different social and political positions and points of view **2** [C] a group of pupils or students taught together

competition 1 [U] the act of trying to win **2** [C] a test of strength, skill, ability, etc.

constraint 1 [U] the condition of hiding one's natural feelings and behavior **2** [C *on*] something that limits one's freedom of action

dread [S] a great fear, esp. of some harm to come

education [S;U] teaching or the training of mind and character

Now read these sentences and choose the correct sentence in each pair.

1. a) There is class of 10-year-olds in that room.
   b) There is a class of 10-year-olds in that room.

2. a) Class is very important in many countries.
   b) A class is very important in many countries.

3. a) The writer thinks competition in school is wrong.
   b) The writer thinks a competition in school is wrong.

4. a) There's spelling competition next week.
   b) There's a spelling competition next week.

5. a) There's always time constraint in school settings.
   b) There's always a time constraint in school settings.

6. a) People often show constraint among strangers.
   b) People often show a constraint among strangers.

7. a) People who have dreads of small places suffer from claustrophobia.
   b) People who have a dread of small places suffer from claustrophobia.

8. a) Parents want their children to get good educations.
   b) Parents want their children to get a good education.

2 Look up these words in your dictionary. Check (✓) the nouns that are both countable and uncountable.

1. air	5. industry
2. company	6. language
3. experience	7. office
4. homework	8. room

Listening

Before listening

1 Discuss the answers to these questions.

1. What was the worst experience you had as an elementary or high school student? What happened? How did the experience make you feel?
2. Who was the best teacher you had when you were in elementary or in high school? Why was this person such a good teacher?
3. How much did your parents help you with your homework? What are the advantages of parents' helping their children with homework? What are the disadvantages?

2 Read the dictionary entries. Why are *perseverance* and *initiative* important in life?

> **i·ni·tia·tive** /ɪˈnɪʃətɪv, -ʃiʲə-/ *n* [U] the ability to make decisions and take action without the help of others
>
> **per·se·ver·ance** /ˌpɜrsəˈvɪərəns/ *n* [U] continual steady effort made to fulfill some aim

You are going to hear a discussion among three people about what children learn by doing homework. How do you think children learn perseverance and initiative by doing homework?

Listening point

3 Listen to the discussion. Write down what children learn by doing homework.

1. _____   3. *perseverance*   5. *initiative*
2. _____   4. _____   6. _____

Comprehension check

4 Listen to the discussion again, and take notes on the points you wrote down in Exercise 3. When you finish, compare notes with another student and add any information you missed.

5 Check (✓) the reasons the mother gives for helping her son with his homework.

1. Her son isn't a good student.
2. She wants to help her son avoid mistakes.
3. Her son has to take a lot of tests.
4. She wants to make difficult material easier for her son.
5. It takes her son a long time to do homework by himself.
6. Her son's teacher punishes him when his homework isn't correct.
7. Her son has a hard teacher.
8. When her son can't do his homework, he gets upset.

What do you think?

6 Discuss the answers to these questions.

1. What do you think the writer of the article on page 73 would think of the opinions expressed in the discussion?
2. Do you agree with everything the speakers told Jeff's mother? With which of their points did you agree or disagree? Why?
3. What would you do if you were a teacher and found out that the father of one of your students was helping her do all of her homework?

Vocabulary check

7 The six words below were used in the discussion. If you cannot remember the context in which they were used, check the tapescript. Then match the definitions in Column A with the words in Column B. (Note: There are six words but only five definitions.)

A	B
1. a person who gives specialist professional advice to others	a) *accomplish*
2. the feeling a person has when annoyed because of disappointment or dissatisfaction	b) *assign*
	c) *challenge*
3. something, often difficult, that requires the full use of a person's abilities or energy for him or her to be successful	d) *consultant*
	e) *frustration*
4. give someone a job to complete	f) *perseverance*
5. finish successfully	

8 Write the derived forms of the *italicized* words. Use a dictionary if you need help.

VERB	NOUN
1. *accomplish*	_____
2. *assign*	_____
3. _____	*challenge*
4. _____	*consultant*
5. _____	*frustration*
6. _____	*perseverance*

9 Which of the words in Exercises 7 and 8 can you relate to your life—past, present, or future?

Example:
I sometimes feel a sense of frustration when I speak English. I know what I want to say, but words just don't seem to come out of my mouth.

77

Language Focus 2

1 Read each pair of sentences. Then answer the questions that follow.

A. The teacher *made* the students *stay* after school.

B. The students *were made to stay* after school.

1. What verb form is used after *made* in sentence **A**?
   a) past tense
   b) base form of the verb
   c) infinitive

2. What verb form is used after *made* in sentence **B**?
   a) present tense
   b) base form of the verb
   c) infinitive

3. Why is there a difference in verb form after *made* in sentences **A** and **B**?

C. It is essential that everybody *be* at the meeting.

D. I recommended that she *see* a consultant about the matter.

4. What verb form is used after *It is essential that* in sentence **C**?
   a) present tense
   b) base form of the verb
   c) infinitive

5. What verb form is used after *I recommended that* in sentence **D**?
   a) present tense
   b) base form of the verb
   c) infinitive

6. What time is referred to in sentence **C**?
   a) past
   b) future

7. What time is referred to in sentence **D**?
   a) past
   b) present

E. I saw a stranger *climb* through the window.

F. I saw a stranger *climbing* through the window.

8. In which sentence, **E** or **F**, did the speaker see the stranger actually enter the building?

Now study the information in the Grammar Box. For further information, read Part 2 of the Language Summary on page 83.

Grammar Box 2

1. The verbs *make* and *let* are followed by an object and the base form of the verb.
   Never *let your schooling get* in the way of your education.
   Teachers *make children do* homework.

To is used after *make* when the verb is passive.
   The children *were made to do* the assignment a second time.

2. Certain verbs and adjective phrases are followed by *that*, a noun or pronoun, and the base form of the verb.
   When Jeff's teacher *requires that he do* an assignment and *that he get* it done on time, it's his responsibility to see that it gets done, not yours.

3. Certain verbs of perception (*see, watch, feel, hear,* etc.) are followed by an object and the base form of the verb or the present participle (verb + *-ing*).
   The writer *has seen friends of his start* helping their children with homework from their very first day in school.
   What would you do if you *saw your child struggling* with difficult material?

2 **Complete these sentences with the correct form of the verbs in parentheses. (Note: Use the passive where necessary.)**

1. All students who arrived late were made _____ (wait) outside.
2. The supervisor didn't let me _____ (enter) because I was five minutes late.
3. The secretary made me _____ (sign) the paper even though she heard me _____ (say) that I didn't understand what I was signing.
4. When we came into the room, we smelled something _____ (burn) and called the fire department.
5. The teacher asked Alicia to leave the room because he saw her _____ (give) the answers by the student next to her.
6. The student insisted that she _____ (allow) another chance to take the test.
7. To be allowed into the examination room, it was essential that you _____ (be) there on time.
8. If she wants to attend this college, it is necessary that she _____ (get) a score of at least 550 on the TOEFL exam.

3 **Use these phrases to talk with another student about what your parents *made* (or *didn't make*) you do and what they *let* (or *didn't let*) you do.**

Example:
Student A: My mother always made me do my homework as soon as I got home from school.
Student B: My parents didn't. They let me do it whenever I wanted.

1. do my homework as soon as I got home from school
2. go out on dates with someone of the opposite sex when I was 14
3. help with the housework
4. stay out late with my friends on school nights
5. go to bed at a certain time when I was in elementary school
6. stay home when I didn't want to go to school
7. eat certain kinds of food
8. go to my room when I was bad
9. smoke cigarettes when I was 15

4 **Read the situations and complete the statements. Then compare answers with other students.**

1. Marco wants to improve his English pronunciation. What do you recommend?
   I recommend that . . .

2. Anita finds it difficult to learn as many new words as she would like. What do you suggest?
   I suggest that . . .

3. Hassan wants to finish his studies at an American university. What does he need to do?
   It's essential that . . .

4. Mr. Tran wants your advice. He does a lot of grammar exercises; but when he writes and speaks English, he still makes a lot of mistakes. What do you advise?
   I advise that . . .

5. Carol Oliveiro teaches English. Last week some of her students were annoyed with something she had done. What had she done to annoy them?
   She had demanded that . . .

6. Some other students of Ms. Oliveiro say that they know they make many mistakes when they talk to each other in groups, but she doesn't correct them. What advice can you give?
   It's important that . . .

Talking Point

A new language school is setting up an English-language course for intermediate-level students. The students will have class three days a week; each class will last two hours. The school would like your advice on how to set up the best course possible for these new students. Work in groups of four or five, and complete the questionnaire. When you finish, compare your group's answers with those of another group.

QUESTIONNAIRE

1. Look at the subject areas below. How much time a week should be spent on each area in a class that meets six hours a week? (Write the amount of time in each blank.)

Grammar _____   Discussions and other
Vocabulary _____   speaking activities _____
Pronunciation _____   Translation _____
Listening comprehension _____   Writing _____
Reading comprehension _____   Spelling _____

2. What is the most important role of the teacher? Rank the areas below in the order of importance (*1* being for the most important and *9* being for the least important).

Answer students' questions _____
Create a fun atmosphere in the classroom _____
Explain English grammar _____
Give students interesting activities to do _____
Go over homework _____
Make students want to learn _____
Read aloud to students _____
Teach pronunciation _____
Teach the meaning of new words _____
Other (Please specify) _____

3. How much time should students spend in each class hour doing the following? (Write the amount of time in each blank.)

Listening to the teacher _____
Working individually _____
Working with another student _____
Working in a group with at least three other students _____

4. When should the teacher NOT correct students' mistakes? (Write **X** in the appropriate blank(s).)

When they are doing a grammar exercise with another student _____
When they are speaking in front of the class _____
When they are having a discussion in a group _____
The teacher should correct all the mistakes students make. _____
Other (Please specify) _____

5. What books should the students have? (Write X in the appropriate blank(s).)

A grammar book _____
A bilingual dictionary _____
A monolingual dictionary _____
A reading book _____
Other (Please specify) _____

6. How much homework should the students be expected to do after each class? (Write X in the appropriate blank.)

None _____
$1/2$ hour _____
1 hour _____
$1 1/2$ hours _____
More than $1 1/2$ hours _____

7. What kind(s) of homework assignments should the students be given? (Write **X** in the appropriate blank(s).)

Grammar exercises _____
Vocabulary memorization _____
Reading assignments
(newspaper and magazine articles, for example) _____
Writing assignments
(letters and compositions, for example) _____
Other (Please specify) _____

8. What were you made to do in previous English classes that these students should not have to do? (Please list.)

_____
_____
_____

9. What other helpful suggestions can you give the school? (Please list.)

_____
_____
_____

Vocabulary Development 2

Stems and affixes

Many words are made up of *stems* (the central part of words) and *affixes* (prefixes and suffixes). Understanding the meaning of parts of words can help you guess the general meaning of a new word.

1 Look at these pairs of words and underline the parts of the two words that are similar.

Examples:
contradiction: a fact that is opposite in nature or character to
contrary: the opposite

1. *contradiction:* the act of saying someone is wrong or untruthful
predict: see or describe a future happening in advance

2. *geography:* the study of the countries of the world and of the seas, rivers, towns, etc., on the earth's surface
telegraph: a method of sending messages along wire by electric signals

3. *meteorology:* the study of weather conditions
psychology: the study of the mind and the way it works

4. *perspective:* the way in which a matter is judged, so that background, future or possible problems, etc., are taken into consideration
spectator: a person who watches (especially an event or sports) without taking part

5. *telescope:* a tubelike scientific instrument which makes distant objects appear nearer and larger
telegraph: a method of sending messages along wire by electric signals

Now read the definitions of the words. Then match each stem and affix in Column A with its meaning in Column B.

A	B
1. contra	a) far
2. dict	b) look at
3. graph	c) opposite
4. ology	d) say
5. spect	e) study of
6. tele	f) write

2 Write down other words you know that contain the stems and affixes in Exercise 1. When you finish, compare words with other students. Be sure you are able to explain the meanings of the words.

1. contra	4. ology
2. dict	5. spect
3. graph	6. tele

Writing

A. Parallel structures

In written English, parallel ideas are expressed in parallel forms.
My students are compelled *to herd* themselves from room to room, *to sit* in daily confinement with other people, and *to hear* me whether or not they are ready.

1 Look at these sentences, which are from this unit's reading, and underline the structures that are parallel.

1. Yet I see no contradiction in coming each day to where young people are and attempting to see to their education.

2. Each year I come to admire many of my students and to like them so well that I am sad to see them go.

3. Yet for all this, it seems to me that many of my students should simply be elsewhere, that they would be better served by a different sort of education, and that their society would be better served by it, too.

4. Evenings are my time for nurturing our children's interest in geography, for discussing the day's news, and for reading poems to them before they go to bed.

2 Complete these sentences with words that are logical and that match in form.

1. My teacher is both understanding and . . .
2. When I study, I never watch TV or . . .
3. Schools are places where students can learn many new things and where . . .
4. You will do well on the test if you answer all the questions and if . . .

3 Correct these sentences so that the structures are parallel. (Note: In some sentences, there is more than one correct answer.)

> **Example:** In my free time, I like reading and to go swimming.
> *In my free time, I like reading and going swimming.*
>   OR
> *In my free time, I like to read and to go swimming.*

1. Doing grammar exercises is easy; to use correct grammar when I speak is difficult.
2. Many people learn a foreign language so that they can study at a foreign university or for business.
3. Traveling abroad is not only fun but you learn a lot.
4. If you do not know the meaning of the word, you should look it up in the dictionary, or why don't you ask the teacher.
5. Children would like school more if they did not have to do homework and teachers should not punish them.

Αντίθετα με την Αγγλική η Ελληνική γλώσσα γράφεται όπως την ακούς.

Bence İngilizce dilinin zorluklarından birisi, birçok kelimelerin birçok değişik anlama gelmesidir.

> ## What difficulties do you have learning English?

Beaucoup de mots se ressemblent mais ne veulent pas dire la même chose

O mais difícil e confuso em inglês para mim é a colocação dos artigos, preposições e conjunções.

太多單字，太多文法，太多俚語，太多時間去学習

Самое странное и трудное в английском языке – английский язык

B. Essay development

A well-written essay in English contains:
- an introductory paragraph.
- main body paragraph one.
- main body paragraph two.
- main body paragraph three.
- a concluding paragraph.

1 Choose nine of the main ideas from the box below that would be appropriate for the three essay topics below. Write your answers in the blanks.

1. Topic: The Pressures of Being a Student
   Introductory paragraph
   Main body paragraph one: _____
   Main body paragraph two: _____
   Main body paragraph three:_____
   Concluding paragraph
2. Topic: The Pressures of Being a Foreign Student
   Introductory paragraph
   Main body paragraph one:_____
   Main body paragraph two:_____
   Main body paragraph three:_____
   Concluding paragraph
3. Topic: The Difficulties of Learning English
   Introductory paragraph
   Main body paragraph one:_____
   Main body paragraph two: _____
   Main body paragraph three:_____
   Concluding paragraph

Main Ideas
a) Competition
b) Culture shock
c) Grading
d) Grammar
e) Homework
f) Language
g) Listening comprehension
h) Loneliness
i) Pronunciation
j) Reading comprehension
k) Talking
l) Testing
m) Time management
n) Vocabulary
o) Writing

2 Write a five-paragraph essay on one of the topics in Exercise 1.

Language Summary

Part 1: Articles (generic or specific reference)

1. The indefinite article (*a* or *an*) for singular count nouns:
The indefinite article is used to talk about a noun that is NOT specified or identified as a particular one.
There's *a student* waiting to see you outside.
We do not know which particular student this is.

2. The definite article (*the*) for a singular or plural count noun or a noncount noun: The definite article is used to talk about a noun that has been specified or identified. A noun is specified or identified when:
a) the noun has been mentioned before.
There's a student waiting to see you. *The student* said you told her to wait.
Here, *the* is used because it is the second time the speaker is referring to the student.

b) the noun is specified in a noun group.
Our present system is not in *the best interests of society*.
Here, *of society* specifies which interests the writer means.

c) the noun is the only one.
It might be on a summer day that we talk about *the sun*.
It is clear which sun is being referred to since there is only one.
"Please erase *the blackboard*," Ms. Flamm said.
Here, the people in the classroom know which blackboard Ms. Flamm is referring to because there is only one.

3. No article (Ø) for a plural count noun or a noncount noun:
No article is used when talking *in general* about people, animals, objects, ideas, etc.
Do *schools* fail *children*?

Problem areas:
a) No article is used in certain expressions with:
bed (for example, *go to bed, be in bed*)
work (for example, *go to work, be at work, start work*)
home (for example, *go home, be at home*)
class (for example, *be in class, go to class*)
    RIGHT: We read poems to our children before they go to bed.
    WRONG: We read poems to our children before they go to the bed.
b) No article is used in certain expressions when the speaker is talking about the place's function as an institution.
school (for example, *go to school, be in school*)
My daughter *goes to school* at 8:00 every morning.
    (She's a student there and goes to learn.)
college (for example, *go to college, be in college*)
I hope my children will be able to *go to college*.
    (I hope they will be able to study in one in the future.)
church (for example, *go to church, be in church*)
Mr. and Mrs. Thompson *are in church*.
    (They are there to pray.)
jail or prison (for example, *go to prison, be in prison*)
He *has been in prison* for five years. (He is a prisoner.)
However, *the* is used when referring to these places as buildings.
I'm going *to the school* to talk to my daughter's teacher.
    (I'm going to the building. I do not study there.)

She's *in the church* waiting for a friend.
    (She's not there to pray.)
The lawyer went *to the prison* to talk to one of the prisoners.   (The lawyer was not there because he was a prisoner.)

Part 2: Verb patterns

In Unit 6, Book A, you saw that certain verbs are followed by a gerund, certain verbs are followed by an infinitive, and certain verbs can be followed by a gerund or an infinitive. This section presents other verb patterns.

1. An object and the base form of the verb is used after *make* and *let*.
Never *let your schooling get* in the way of your education.
Teachers *make children do* homework.
To is used after *make* when the verb is passive.
The children *were made to do* the assignment a second time.
(*Let* is not used in the passive when it means "to allow.")
The students were allowed to leave early.

2. *That* + a noun (or pronoun) + the base form of the verb is used after certain verbs and adjective phrases.*
When Jeff's teacher *requires that he do* an assignment and *that he get* it done on time, it's his responsibility to see that it gets done, not yours.

When children are doing homework, the writer *recommends that their parents learn* to be consultants rather than participants.

It is important *that Jeff not get* help from you when he does his homework.

* For a list of these verbs and adjective phrases, see page 92.

3. An object + the base form of the verb *or* an object + present participle (verb-*ing*) is used after certain verbs of perception (*see, watch, feel, hear,* etc.).
The writer *has seen friends of his start* helping their children with homework from their very first day in school.

What would you do if you *saw your child struggling* with difficult material?

Sometimes, as in the sentences above, there is little difference in meaning between the two forms. Other times there is a clear difference between the base form of the verb and the present participle.
I *saw that group of students come* to registration.

The base form of the verb refers to the complete action. (When I saw them, they had already entered the room where registration was taking place.)
I saw *that group of students coming* to registration.

The present participle refers to an action in progress. (When I saw them, they were on their way to the room where registration was taking place. However, I didn't see them in the room.)

Tapescript
Unit One
Listening

Page 7, Exercises 2 and 3

Man: Why is it that we always think new means better? I don't know about you but I reckon we've been tricked for years into thinking we can buy all kinds of things which will help us all solve all our problems and which, when you sit down and think about it carefully, haven't really changed anything at all. We are no better off than we were before we bought these things. In fact, we're worse off because we've spent good money for a delusion.

Look at Edison, for example. You've heard of Thomas Edison? Thanks to him we have the light bulb. Do we read any more as a result? If we do, our eyes probably don't last as long as they used to. What about that? Think about it.

Then there are microwave ovens. Just about everyone I know has one. Have microwave ovens improved the taste of the food we eat?

And what about video recorders? So we can record one bad TV program while we're watching another bad one. Big deal. Two bad programs for the price of one.

Here I sit next to my computer, where I compose clever words like these. Years ago, when I was in college, I typed out my clever words on my mother's old manual typewriter. It was slow and tedious. When I got my first job, I moved up the gadget ladder and promoted myself to an electric typewriter. I thought I had found paradise. Paradise? I don't even know where my electric typewriter is anymore. Now I can't imagine writing anything on a typewriter, let alone with a pen. A pen? Do you remember pens? But the real question is this: Has my computer made me a better writer? Quicker maybe, but better? I doubt it. I'd be the same writer if I were still using that old manual typewriter, or, heaven forbid, a pen.

And another thing ... I can't imagine life without my pocket calculator? But am I really better off with it? Years ago I used to be able to multiply, divide, and find percentages in my head. Now I don't trust myself to add or subtract. I don't even try. Instead, I run to my desk drawer to get my calculator. And what do I do if I see something on sale at a store and have to figure out what one third of four hundred and eighty-five dollars and ninety-nine cents is? I panic. I think about running home to get my calculator, but then I run the risk that this bargain may not be there when I get back. So I search franti-

cally for a pencil and paper and try to remember how to do what I was so good at doing in elementary school. I can't help but wonder what the pocket calculator has done to my brain.

One more thing. For years I had a real wristwatch, you know, one with a minute hand, a second hand, and numbers around the face. Sometimes I forgot to wind it, and sometimes it gained or lost a few minutes. Sometimes I got to places a bit late. But a lot of the time I got to places early. I've now got a quartz watch. I never have to touch it. It just goes on and on and will probably live longer than I will. Just imagine the world when human civilization has been wiped out. All those quartz watches keeping perfect time for ever and ever and nobody around to tell the time from them anymore. Anyway, do they help us get to appointments on time? They do not. On average we're probably less punctual than we used to be. Which reminds me . . . I'm late for my next appointment. I wish I had a gadget that could whisk me from one place to another without all the hassle . . . or do I?

Unit Two
Listening

Page 20, Exercise 2; Page 21, Exercise 3

Commercial One:
A hundred years ago people used to say "A man's home is his castle." Now with the new Home Mood Sensor, your home will be your friend. Once the Home Mood Sensor - Arthur is what it likes to be called - detects your mood, it will take care of your every need, right down to the precise amount of caffeine you will need in your morning coffee. If you're happy, you'll get decaffeinated coffee. If you're upset, regular coffee will be ready and waiting. Now, you're saying to yourself, this is a gimmick. It can't be so. Not even people who have known me for years can understand my mood. But your Home Mood Sensor will know you in ways that friends and relatives never do. It will be able to tell if you're depressed by how long you stay in the shower, how hot the water is, and whether you're singing or whistling. It will know if you're angry by the way you walk in the door. If you are, it will cool the room or switch on soothing music without your ever noticing. Arthur will be a true friend, providing you with protection, too. When you're out of town, Arthur will make people believe someone is at home by slamming doors, turning lights on and off, and playing tapes of children screaming and even a husband and wife arguing. If Arthur senses an intruder, it will broadcast the sound of a large dog barking. Arthur has so much to offer. You must be wondering how you could have lived without a

friend like this for so long. Don't wonder a moment longer.

Commercial Two:
Here it is. The car of your dreams. The perfect car. Perfection. You will wonder how you managed before . . . without Perfection. (*Sound of a car running into another.*) Dents all over the place? Thousands of dollars to make your car look new again? Well, kiss those days goodbye. With Perfection's sleek, plastic body you'll never see a dent again and that's a promise. And no more rust, not even after twenty years. With Perfection you'll never need a tune-up again. And that's just the beginning. Perfection is loaded with electronic options that are astounding. When it has mechanical trouble, microchips will tell your mechanic just what's wrong. The on-board navigation system will make it impossible for you to get lost. Just locate your position on a color video map display located on the passenger side of the car, and the display with its atlas of maps stored on a videodisc will give directions on the best way to get where you're going. If you break down out in the desert, or somewhere less exotic, the car will transmit an emergency call to a watching satellite. And if you're worried that you may have drunk too much to drive home? The alcohol detector will prevent you from starting up if you've had too many drinks for the road. Most importantly, because there's nothing more important than your life, Perfection's artificial intelligence provides automatic collision avoidance. When Perfection sees that a car is about to hit you, it will on its own, before you yourself are aware of anything, brake or steer itself out of the impending disaster. With all this and a car that gets over a hundred miles per gallon, is there any question that Perfection's here? And that is just the beginning . . .

Commercial Three:
Feeling tense and jittery? Having trouble sleeping? Problems at school getting you down? Exhausted by it all? Maybe you should try a session in the new Purpose 1 relaxation chair. This isn't just any armchair. It's wired to a computer that magically calls up music, lights, voices, and even smells – all of which are designed to relax your body and calm your mind. As you sink down into the chair's soft cushions, the lights in the room slowly dim. Above your head, a light begins blinking rhythmically – on . . . off . . . on . . . off. You can see flashes of light even with your eyes closed. You can hear voices, but you can't make out what they're saying. Sometimes you catch a few words, but most of the message seems garbled. After a while, you give up trying to listen. You notice that the arms of the chair are moving very slowly – up and down, up and down. And you're breathing in just the same

rhythm. Your body feels so heavy you wonder whether you could even lift one finger. Then, in the distance, you hear the sound of ocean waves. A gentle breeze blows your hair. You can even smell the ocean spray. A soft voice whispers "You're walking along a beach. The sand feels warm under your bare feet ..." The next thing you know, someone is tugging at your arm. "Time to go," she says. "You must have fallen asleep." You get out of the chair, all your troubles have faded away, and you are ready to get on with the rest of your day.

Commercial Four:
"Come on, you can run faster than that! If you're going to be an Olympic champion, you're going to have to try harder." That's not your coach nagging you—it's the new Pro Coach computer. In its memory, it has all kinds of information about you. It knows how efficiently your body uses oxygen and how powerful your muscles are. It knows all about your body build, your reflexes, and how fast you respond when you see or hear something. It uses this information to design a training program especially for you. As you practice, it lets you know how you're doing. It even warns you if you're overdoing it—or scolds you if you're being lazy. These computers will make sure you get in shape. To order one, call up the Discount Shopping Service on your home computer now, and you'll be on your way to better body conditioning within hours.

Language Focus 2

Page 23, Exercise 1

Announcer: Fran, who lives in the U.S., has reserved a seat on a charter flight to Ireland. She's calling her friend, Chris, in Ireland, to talk to him about her travel plans.

Chris: Hello?

Fran: Hi, Chris. This is Fran.

Chris: Hi. Did you get my message?

Fran: Uh-huh. I got some more information from the charter company, but they still can't tell me exactly what time we'll be leaving here.

Chris: Well, at least they must know whether the arrival is scheduled for the morning, afternoon, or evening . . .

Fran: The representative told me we'll be arriving in the evening.

Chris: That's good because I won't have returned from the teachers' conference in Dublin until midday. When will they let you know the exact time?

Fran: Two days before the flight. So why don't I call

you the Friday before the flight around 3 o'clock your time?

Chris: No, that won't be any good. I'll have left for the conference by then. How about if I call you before I leave, say around 2 o'clock. That'll be 9 o'clock your time.

Fran: No, that's no good. I'll be teaching at 9. Look, don't worry about it. When I get out of customs, I'll call you, and if nobody answers, I'll assume you've already left for the airport.

Chris: That's probably best. So then I'll see you sometime next Sunday.

Fran: Okay. See you then. Bye.

Chris: Bye.

Unit Three
Listening

Page 36, Exercise 2

(Introductory skit)

Page 36, Exercise 2 and 3

We faked this opening a little. All these things did happen yesterday but certainly not in the course of a minute. We're playing it to illustrate that the pace of life for many of us in this society has become incredibly rushed.

When I think about growing up and my parents' generation, I begin to realize that things have speeded up drastically. My parents both worked during much of my youth but they still had time for dinners, for slow conversations over a morning cup of coffee with a neighbor or with friends. My father is 86 and he still works a bit. When I look at his home, and as a psychiatrist he's not poor, and when I look at the home of my 90-year-old aunt, the first thing I notice is that there's just not a lot of stuff in it, and it hasn't changed much over five, ten years. There's no computer, no fax machine. The phones have rotary dials. The television is old, and in my aunt's house it's still black and white. In the evening my father plays chess, or reads, or works on a lecture.

Almost no new m-material possessions enter or leave the house. Possessions in some way that I don't really understand eat into time. In my apartment the phone is always ringing, packages are always appearing, letters that have to be opened and responded to. Every moment is used often for two or three things at once and is never enough. About six months ago I interviewed an anthropologist who was studying East and West Berlin. He said that when unification came to the East, time speeded up fourfold. The East Germans suddenly had no time for their friends. They had to learn how

to hustle to write their resumes. They spent much more time in consumption. We celebrated the freedom of choice they gained, the freedom of the marketplace, the hundreds of brands of this and that, but no words were spent, nor could we even conceive of the freedoms they might have lost, the freedom of time. Americans, I learned today in *The Washington Post*, consume twice as much as forty years ago, and yet almost every middle-class person I know is angry because they're overextended with mortgage payments, car payments, credit card debt and are much less free to maneuver than their parents, who did more with less. My aunt has never had a credit card, and she still relies on checks and cash. She lives in an apartment that has never had a mortgage payment. I notice that my father also never uses credit cards. They both seem to have an abundance of time. Slow, reflective time is disappearing, even for college students. When I was in college, no one I knew kept a date book. There were classes and studying and parties and long, slow talks in cafes, discussions until 2 A.M. about metaphysical questions. Most of the students I meet today have date books and every hour is quantified. Even younger children are pushed from activity to activity. I remember long, slow summers spending days exploring an old, abandoned house, just wandering, walking with friends on the beach, and now of course there's all this talk of making the school year even longer, perhaps a boon to working parents living in unsafe areas. But it's frightening that no one is talking about the other option, making parents' vacations longer, like in West Germany. Their six weeks vacation doesn't seem to have affected their productivity. I once read that in the Middle Ages half of the year was devoted to holidays. I'm not saying that technology is all to blame. Some technology does free us, like answering machines, which allow us to censor our calls and pretend we're out when we're really at home, freeing up private space. I've avoided many a person and even news assignments that way. Shh, don't tell National Public Radio. But other new devices seem to have their own relentless logic. The fax machine makes people assume a deadline is really a deadline. Things no longer can get conveniently lost in the mail. The old trick is no longer possible. You say you're sending it out today and then after three days more work you drop it by hand at their door. I've woken up some mornings longing to live a hundred years ago when people simply set aside a day for receiving visitors. I long for the weekly newspaper. And here's another heresy for journalists. Do we really have to know the news the hour that it happens?

Language Focus 3

Page 37, Exercise 1

Oh, God, where's that report? I know. I must have put it in my briefcase. No, it's not here. I must've left it at home. Let me call Steve. If he hurries, he can get it here in 20 minutes. Where is he? Oh, it's 8:30. He must be taking the children to school. Oh, God, what am I going to do? The meeting starts in half an hour. What am I going to tell Mr. Morrison?

Unit Four
Listening

Page 49, Exercise 3

Announcer: Hearing about archaeologists excavating to find ruins of ancient Egyptian civilization or searching for the earliest ancestors of humankind in Africa would not surprise most of our listeners, but would you be surprised to learn that there is an archaeologist who digs up rubbish dumps? Professor Mark Reynold has been doing just that for the past 15 years. He joins us from his office at Royal College in Kansas . . . Professor Reynold, thank you for being with us.

Reynold: Hi, how are you? It's a pleasure to be here.

Announcer: How does an archaeologist who used to dig up ancient burial sites in Central America get interested in excavating other people's trash?

Reynold: Well, it was actually two of my students about 16 years ago who inspired me. For their class project they decided to study trash in different areas of Springfield to see what could be learned from the contents of people's trashcans. I thought it was such a great idea that I've been going through trash ever since.

Announcer: What is it you have learned about people from this type of research?

Reynold: Well, first of all, people waste far more than they claim. For example, I've discovered that 10 to 20% of fresh food is thrown away. When there is a shortage of food in the world, it's amazing how much is thrown away. 13 years ago when there was a national beef shortage and beef was hard to find, the amount of beef in Springfield's trash cans tripled.

Announcer: How do you account for that?

Reynold: It was the result of panic buying. People bought as much as they could, but they bought cheap cuts, which they did not know how to cook, and they bought so much that some of it went bad.

Announcer: What else have you learned?

Reynold: I've also discovered that people buy less healthy food than they claim, and that there are few truly healthy eaters. Along with the high-grain bread wrappers, which there are always plenty of, we usually find the remains of gooey pastries and candy wrappers too.

Announcer: And now you've moved on from trash-cans to landfills?

Reynold: Yes. Since political forces are always arguing over the need to reduce the amount of trash going into America's landfills, I decided to find out what the landfills contained.

Announcer: What are they crammed with – polystyrene, fast-food packaging, and disposable diapers?

Reynold: No, surprisingly no. Polystyrene accounts for 0.33% of the volume of a typical landfill; fast-food packaging for 0.25% and disposable diapers for 1.8%. All plastics account for some 12% of landfill waste. The fastest-growing component of landfills in this country is paper. It now takes up roughly half the space. Telephone directories take up an especially large amount of space. Building waste accounts for a further 20%.

Announcer: How is it that you're able to find all this?

Reynold: Unfortunately, the worst news is that rubbish in modern landfills hardly rots because they are too well-sealed and as a result too dry. As proof of this, about five years ago, when I was excavating a landfill outside of New York City I found a head of lettuce that was at least five years old but looked better than many do after a week in the refrigerator.

Announcer: How can you tell how old a head of lettuce is?

Reynold: It's easier to date material than one might think since the landfills are filled with well-preserved newspapers!

Announcer: So what is popularly thought of as biodegradable is usually well preserved?

Reynold: Exactly. For that reason, I don't understand why environmentalists so strongly promote biodegradable plastics made with cornstarch. That bugs in a landfill won't eat corn on the cob is a known fact, so if they won't eat the corn on the cob, what makes environmentalists think the bugs will eat corn-starch in plastics?

Announcer: What of hazardous waste? Have you found evidence that that too is dumped?

Reynold: Yes. Though companies spend a lot of time and money searching for legal ways to dispose of their hazardous waste, I've turned up lots of hazardous waste from city trash cans . . . Cans of motor oil, you name it. If you bought fingernail polish in 55-gallon drums, you couldn't throw it away in a regular American rubbish dump. But we get 570,000 bottles of fingernail polish every year in Springfield. When we dig it up 30 years later, you could still unscrew the cap and paint your nails with it.

Announcer: I understand, Professor Reynold, that you're off to Portland to dig up three landfills there.

Reynold: Yes. Portland's of particular interest to me because the city has run a curbside recycling scheme for several years. I'm curious to learn how much separated trash ends up not recycled, but on the same pile with everything else.

Announcer: Professor Reynold, thank you for being with us.

Reynold: I thank you.

Announcer: Mark Reynold, professor of archaeology, speaking with us from his office at Royal College in Kansas.

Unit Five
Language Focus 1

Page 60, Exercise 4

Makulo Tatu: New York's the worst place I've ever been to. The city is dirty and noisy. Sure it's an interesting place, but I've been to lots of interesting places around the world, and I had a much better time than I had in New York. I'm telling you I've never met such rude and unfriendly people. One day while I was walking along Fifth Avenue, I stopped and asked this man for directions. In most places, people are happy to help a stranger, but not in New York. Do you know what he said? "Who cares?" I'm getting married later in the year and my fiancée's dream has always been to go to New York. I love her very much and I'd do just about anything for her. But one thing's for sure: We're not going to New York. I'll never go to New York again, not for all the money in the world!

Carla Pirovano: Oh, New York, I can't say enough about the place. I've been there four times, and each time I go there I like it even more than before. I get a great sense of excitement as soon as the plane lands there because it's a city that never sleeps. I also love being in a place where I can meet people from all over the world. And if you love jazz, then New York's definitely the place to be. I know it's dangerous, but as long as a person's careful, noth-

ing will happen. I've traveled a lot, but I've really never been to a place where I've had so much fun. The last time I was there I hardly had time to sleep. There were so many places to go and so many things to see. If you haven't ever been to New York, you really should take a trip there. Oh, I promise you, you won't be sorry.

Listening

Page 62, Exercise 2

1. I took pity on the young man because he looked like he badly needed help.
2. She looked at me sympathetically. I thought that if I asked her to help me, she would agree to do so.
3. It was five o'clock in the morning. Dawn was breaking, and I could see through the window that it was getting light.
4. The suitcases were so heavy that I couldn't lift them. All I could do was drag them.
5. You gave me your word, and I was depending on you. How can you break your promise now when I need you?
6. When I realized how late I was, I dashed out of the room.
7. I was relieved when I got there a few minutes early because I'd been worried that I would be late.
8. I can't find the place on the map so I can't say for sure, but instinct tells me that this is the right way.

Listening

Page 62, Exercise 3

It was spring, springtime in Paris, a time for love, romance, and adventure and, I hoped, an ideal occasion to enroll at the Institut and to combine all of this with improving my French. You can only really learn by going there, they said. But there was another side to Paris in spring that I hadn't given as much attention to as I should have before setting off from England. Now, having learned my lesson the hard way, I know better. Never go to Paris in the spring without being sure of where you're going to spend your first night. Unless, of course, you consider that traipsing up and down with heavy suitcases which rip your arms out of their sockets is all part of the fun. Or that doing without a night's sleep is a small price to pay for the chance to call yourself a true traveler.

In spite of a delayed boat arrival on the French coast, and an even more delayed train, neither of these possibilities was part of my expectations as my train pulled into the Gare du Nord during the early hours of the morning. I had not managed to catch any sleep, but was quite sure I would soon make up for this even if the most convenient hotel

In spite of a delayed boat arrival on the French coast, and an even more delayed train, neither of these possibilities was part of my expectations as my train pulled into the Gare du Nord during the early hours of the morning. I had not managed to catch any sleep, but was quite sure I would soon make up for this even if the most convenient hotel turned out to be less than I would have normally accepted. After all, there would be hundreds of hotels to choose from.

Sadly, this was not to be. Not only were the first five I tried fully booked, but the student night porter in the last one seemed to delight in telling me that I wouldn't find a bed in the whole of Paris without a reservation. It is amazing how unhelpful Parisians can be, particularly student night porter Parisians at three o'clock in the morning, confronted with a foolish and rather bad-tempered Englishman.

At the next one, however, an elderly lady concierge took pity on me. She sat in genteel decay at her desk. Wreathed in cigarette smoke, she stood up with an effort and smiled sympathetically. She had no rooms free but said she would be willing to take care of my luggage while I tried two more hotels nearby which would probably have beds to spare. Not in the same class as her establishment, she warned, but clean and inexpensive. As I looked around at the peeling wallpaper and dark, uninviting staircase, I could only wonder how bad the conditions might get. Nevertheless, I needed to put my body and my bags down somewhere, so I thanked her warmly and left with renewed hope.

The young African receptionist in the next hotel peered at me sleepily. Yes, he had a room, though it took me a while to impress on him the here and now interpretation of "tonight" and that I would be shortly returning with my suitcases. For one hundred and fifty francs, I couldn't expect much, but all I needed was a place to put my head.

Dawn was breaking by the time I arrived back at the hotel, dragging my luggage the last few yards up to the reception. My young receptionist had been replaced by another, more senior. I waited patiently for him to look up and smiled when he did so. The smile was not returned. "Pas de chambres," he said. I explained as best I could that there was certainly some kind of mistake. The younger man, after all, had said it would be alright and surely they couldn't have given the room to someone else in the time that I had been away. It was nothing as complicated as that, however. There was just not a room. The younger man was called and after half an hour of discussion between them, it turned out that the younger man had made a mistake. He

shouldn't have said there was a room since the hotel had been fully booked for a week. But he had given his word and Monsieur l'Anglais had to have a room for the night or what was left of it. The younger man accordingly offered me the use of his room, but I accepted instead the use of the hotel breakfast room. As the first guests appeared for breakfast, refreshed and ready to meet the day, I could only wonder if the fight for my prize had been worth it.

I had not slept and I gave up the struggle at about seven. My room, I learned, would be ready as soon as a Monsieur Farouk had checked out, so I ventured out once more into the real world of the tenth *arrondissement*, resolving also to get some rest before enrolling at the Institut for the next day's classes. The city had come to life, even if I hadn't. Cars hooted, people argued, little old ladies were going about their daily shopping routines. I set about exploring the neighborhood.

In my room, some hours later, the effects of the journey and a light lunch caught up with me. I fell into a deep contented sleep still wearing the day's clothes but, reassured that my enrolment at the Institut the next morning was too far away to be a cause of concern for the moment.

I woke up with a start, vaguely aware that I had been troubled by dreams of epic proportions, my head throbbing. I looked at my watch. Half past seven. Although it would take less than half an hour to get to the Institut, I wanted to be there in advance. At least I didn't have to get dressed, though the thought of arriving in clothes I had traveled and slept in all night was disconcerting. I splashed my face with water, ran the razor round it once, cleaned my teeth and dashed out, grabbing my briefcase. My African friend was still dozing behind the counter.

The streets were already bustling with activity, pedestrians and cars coming from all angles as I raced along, dodging in between them. I reached the Institut just before eight and was surprised to see the doors weren't opened yet. I was relieved to see no sign of foreign students pushing to get in first, which I had been warned to expect. I smiled triumphantly; at least, I would be the first. I leaned against the outside wall and relaxed, thinking of the work ahead.

By ten past eight, there was still no sign of life at the Institut. I checked the address and the date for registration. What were they up to? This was really quite inexcusable, when people like me had taken so much trouble to come on time and from so far. I walked up to the nearest street corner and back down again. Nearly half past eight. Anger and frustration welled up inside me as I looked around in vain for a sign of possible help or just someone with whom I could share my plight. But no one seemed interested or even curious.

It was then that very slowly the unnerving thought entered my mind. What day was it, in fact? Could it be eight-thirtyish in the evening? Could I have slept only a few hours instead of all through the night? It was a strange feeling. I tried hard to be rational. I looked again around me. Were all these people going to work or going home? Were the shops closed for the night or not yet open? This was crazy. Here I was in the middle of Paris and I didn't even know what day it was. And, I couldn't just walk up to someone and ask them if it was Monday or Tuesday.

Instinct told me it was in fact the evening. But I had to be sure. A strange sort of curiosity came over me. I sat down on a wooden bench underneath a tree, and I watched the world go by, comforted by the thought that I had a whole night's sleep ahead of me . . . Maybe. I still kept an eye on the sky, to see if it got darker or lighter.

Unit Six
Listening

Page 77, Exercise 3 and 4

Pat: God, I'm so tired. I didn't get to do any work on my report until late last night because I had to help Jeff with his homework.

Marilyn: Again? You're always helping him with his homework. Is it his homework or your homework? Don't you think he'd be better off if you let him do it by himself? It is his responsibility, not yours.

Pat: I know but the teacher he has this year is very hard-going. She makes the class do very difficult assignments.

Larry: I don't want to get involved in this, but does Jeff have any learning problems?

Pat: No, he's a good student.

Larry: Then why does he need so much help just because an assignment is difficult?

Marilyn: You know, Pat, I was reading an article the other day just about this subject, about parents getting caught in the homework trap. The writer, a family psychologist, has seen parents, friends of his, actually start helping their children with homework from their very first day in school, and believe it or not, this continued in some cases until their children were in college. He wonders what it is about today's parents that makes them think their children can't manage without them. Did your parents help you as much as you help Jeff?

Pat: No, they never helped. They didn't have the time, but that doesn't mean I wouldn't have wanted them to.

Marilyn: But you did fine in school without their help. Now don't you think Jeff can do as well without help from you?

Pat: Sure, but why should Jeff make mistakes when I can help him avoid them?

Marilyn: To tell you the truth, I think your basic problem is that you want Jeff to be perfect and you have this obsessive fear that he'll make mistakes.

Pat: I wouldn't call it an obsession. What mother wants her children to fail?

Larry: Making mistakes is not failing. Don't you think that people learn from making mistakes?

Pat: Sure, but why should he suffer disappointment when he doesn't need to?

Marilyn: Because that's what he's going to face throughout his life. Isn't school supposed to prepare children for what they're going to face in life?

Larry: It seems to me that teachers make children do homework so they have an opportunity to practice and strengthen academic skills. That way they'll get better grades when they're tested on the material.

Pat: I don't want my child to go through life thinking school is about tests and grades.

Larry: But that's the reality in school. And you're not there when he has his tests.

Marilyn: Look at matters from the teacher's perspective. They want to see from the homework they assign how much their students have learned. If you've done even only part of that work, Jeff's teacher won't learn the truth until the test.

Larry: Anyway, homework isn't only about academic learning, about mastering required material. It teaches responsibility.

Marilyn: That's what I was saying before. When Jeff's teacher requires that he do an assignment and that he get it done on time, it's his responsibility to see that it gets done, not yours. He has to learn to be responsible for his successes as well as his mistakes. If you always take over Jeff's responsibilities, when will he learn that when the ball's in his court he's got to pick it up and do something with it?

90

Pat: Well, that's all well and true, but what would *you* do if you saw your child struggling with difficult material that was making him miserable?

Larry: I can tell you one thing: with three children in our house, we saw that all the time. But what they learned from such challenges was perseverance, that no matter what difficulties there are, they should finish what they set out to do, to accomplish. We would encourage them, say, "Come on, you can do it. We know you can." But I don't think either of us ever thought it was our job to protect the kids from frustration. If you do that, how will they cope with the frustration they're sure to face in their adult life? Jeff won't always be able to come home to you when he's got something difficult to do that he can't do. You may think you're making his life easier, but what you're really doing is making his life in the future more difficult.

Pat: And what about all the time it takes? When I'm not home at night to help Jeff, he's up until midnight getting his homework done.

Marilyn: But maybe that's because most of the time you're organizing his time for him. He's not learning what the writer of this article called "time management," to organize his time in an effective manner so that he can get things done on time and do them well. If you told him his homework had to be finished by say, nine o'clock, I bet after a while, if you gave him the chance, he'd manage. And don't tell him when to start. It should be his job to organize his time so that he finishes by nine. If he can do it by starting at eight, that's fine. If not, then he'd just have to learn to start at seven.

Larry: And letting him decide what time to start his homework in order to meet your deadline will teach him initiative too. He'll learn to think about what his goals are and how to achieve them. If you're always assuming initiative for Jeff, how will he ever develop the ability for himself?

Pat: And when he says he can't do it?

Larry: Encourage him. He needs self-confidence. Your being in the trap of doing his homework with him probably teaches him just the opposite – that you have no confidence in him, that you don't think he can do the work without you. He ends up with no confidence in himself, and you know as well as I

do that that's no way to go through life.

Pat: No, I want Jeff to have a high opinion of his self-worth. I don't want him to think that I don't trust his abilities or that he's incapable.

Larry: So then, take yourself out of the game. Learn to watch from the sidelines instead. Be a spectator, not a participant. In the beginning it might be as difficult for you to adjust to this new role as it will be for Jeff, but I'm sure in the end it'll pay off.

Marilyn: Why don't you try taking the advice of the psychologist who wrote the article? He recommends that parents learn to be consultants rather than participants. Show your concern and if Jeff requests some help, don't refuse him, but make sure that what you do doesn't last more than a few minutes.

Pat: It's easier said than done, but I'll try and keep your advice in mind.

Verb Patterns

Common verbs followed by a gerund

admit	discuss	quit
appreciate	dislike	recall
avoid	enjoy	recommend
can't help[1]	escape	resent
can't stand	keep[3]	resist
complete	mention	resume
consider[2]	mind	stop
delay	miss	suggest
deny	postpone	tolerate
detest	practice	understand

Common verbs followed by a gerund or an infinitive (difference in meaning)

forget	regret	stop
mean	remember	try

Common verbs followed by an infinitive

afford	deserve	prepare
agree	fail	promise
appear	hesitate	refuse
arrange	hope	seem
care	learn	struggle
claim	manage	threaten
decide	offer	wait
demand	pretend	wish

Common verbs followed by a gerund or an infinitive (little difference in meaning)

advise	hate	prefer
begin	like	start
continue	love	

Common verbs with or without a pronoun/noun and an infinitive

ask	choose	need
beg	expect	want

Common verbs followed by a pronoun/noun and an infinitive

allow	force	persuade
cause	hire	remind
compel	instruct	require
convince	invite	tell
encourage	order	urge
forbid	permit	warn

Common verbs followed by *that* and a noun clause

assume	guess	recognize
believe	hear[5]	report
confess	indicate	reveal
confirm	know	see[7]
declare	learn[6]	show
demonstrate	maintain	state
estimate	presume	suppose
feel[4]	prove	think

Common verbs and phrases followed by *that* and a noun clause with the base form of the verb

advise	propose	It is essential
ask	recommend	It is important
demand	request	It is necessary
insist	suggest	It is vital

[1] can't help: have no control over
[2] consider: think about
[3] keep: persist in
[4] feel: think
[5] hear: be informed
[6] learn: be informed, discover
[7] see: realize